REFERENCE MATERIALS ON MEXICAN AMERICANS:

An Annotated Bibliography

by

Richard D. Woods

The Scarecrow Press, Inc.

Metuchen, N.J.   1976

Library of Congress Cataloging in Publication Date

Woods, Richard Donovon.
    Reference materials on Mexican Americans.

    Includes indexes.
    1. Reference books--Mexican Americans.   2.   Mexican
Americans--Bibliography.   I.   Title.
E184. M5W66   016. 973'04'6872   76-10663
ISBN 0-8108-0963-X

CONTENTS

iii

INTRODUCTION

Since 1960, much has been written on Mexican Americans. Although their culture dates back to 1846, to pre-Columbian and colonial Mexico, and to the Iberian Peninsula, only recently have Chicanos been the focus of both scholarly and imaginative studies. Prior to 1960, their literature was best exemplified in journalism and in the oral tradition of folklore.

Now the corpus of Mexican-American studies increases through research and through discovery of earlier works pertinent to this culture. The interest in and growth of Chicano materials is reflected in bibliographies, dictionaries, archives, genealogical records, collective biographies and directories. Although bibliographies predominate, most are characterized by hurried compilations, i.e., showing no annotations, capricious selectivity in regard to Mexico and an absence of introductory guidelines for the reader. The other types of reference materials, at times uneven in quality, correspond to the embryonic development in various aspects of Chicanismo. The major deficiencies are in reference-type materials in the humanities--there are now only four in literature and one in the visual arts. Furthermore, there does not exist an encompassing work similar to the Negro Almanac.

However, at this point it is imperative to collect and evaluate all obtainable reference-type works pertinent to the Mexican American; show the researcher or the layman what tools exist; and point out lacunae to which scholarly effort might be directed. For with the recent proliferation of Chicano-related writings, we now have a sufficient body of material which may be labeled reference type--monographs or pamphlets with highly concentrated data with ease of access or works "... which are compiled to supply definite pieces of information of varying extent and intended to be referred to rather than read through" (L. M. Harrod, The Librarian's Glossary, p. 228). Consequently, only works in agreement with the above definition were incorporated into this bibliography.

The types of reference works that qualified for inclusion according to this definition: (a) are dedicated entirely to Mexican-American materials, (b) have a multiethnic perspective with at least one section dealing totally with Chicanos, (c) encompass a theme of the Mexican American though not referring to him specifically, e.g., migrant education, poverty in the United States, etc., or (d) contain references to Chicanos, such as guides to periodical literature and abstracts.

I do not labor over a definition of the ethnic terms, Chicano, Hispano, Latin American, la raza, and Mexicans in the United States, but I usually opt for "Mexican American" because it seems best to embrace the materials I examined. Notwithstanding that the term "Chicano" has topicality reflecting a status of awareness or even belligerency, it is almost a misnomer to refer to Spanish newspapers in 19th-century Louisiana as Chicano or the early Spanish settlers of New Mexico as Chicanos. Therefore, Mexican American is a modus operandi, imperfect and not intended to disparage the Chicano movement.

A second consideration, geographical limits, made me decide in favor of limiting coverage to the continental United States. Since Chicano roots go back to Mexico, little in that country can legitimately be excluded when studying the Mexican American. However, to incorporate reference type material about Mexico would have extended this study to unpublishable lengths; consequently, I have admitted only those references from Mexico which deal directly with the United States and the minority group under consideration, e.g., a title on Arizona in the archives of Mexico City could therefore rightfully be an entry in the bibliography. For those who would deplore my perhaps cavalier treatment of Mexico, I can suggest that they refer to Charles C. Griffin's Latin America; A Guide to the Historical Literature (University of Texas Press, 1971) or some other bibliography dedicated solely to Mexican culture. Because of the universality of Griffin's work, it would be senseless to attempt to duplicate it.

First I tried to limit my study to monographs, but I soon discovered that this would exclude many short but invaluable bibliographies. Therefore, the only stipulation was that the work be published separately, be it only three pages in length. All analytics or bibliographies appended to books and to periodical articles were omitted. Since the Chicano experience is often related through multimedia, I have included guides not only to print materials but also films, filmstrips, tapes, kits, etc.

In these studies I often point out that a lack of proper organization adversely affects use; therefore, so as not to be guilty of the deficiencies I have noted in other studies, I provide three indexes in anticipation of user needs: the author index, both personal and corporate; the subject index, including references and cross references to almost all topics mentioned in my evaluation of 387 works; and finally the title index, self-explanatory.

This bibliography is oriented toward the scholar and the academic library; yet surely its practicality can be extended to both public and school libraries and also to individuals and organizations concerned with the Mexican American. First, it suggests the breadth of the field in both research and programs devoted to understanding and aiding the Mexican American. Second, it can serve as a catalog to librarians who will wish to improve their reference holdings on Mexican Americans. To reach both the academic and the larger public, I analyzed each work herein from the point of view of purpose, scope, arrangement, and evaluation.

Alphabetical by author surname, the entries are tied together by a syndetic index that substitutes for categorization by discipline within the bibliography. A Dewey-type classification of material was rejected in favor of an integrated list, since it would have allowed for little flexibility, necessitated arbitrary decisions as to placement of certain works, and over-emphasized lacunae in several fields.

Although I attempted to include everything pertinent, subject to the above-mentioned criteria, I doubtlessly missed works of high value. Their omission is due to unavailability, nonexistence at the time of this compilation, or my own lack of awareness of them. I hope that this bibliography will be a resource tool. May it also be seminal in the generation of more reference-type works on the Chicanos.

THE BIBLIOGRAPHY

1 Abraham, Pauline. Bibliography: Indians of North America, Mexican Americans, Negroes--Civil Rights. An
Annotated List. South Bend: Indiana University at
South Bend, 1974. 50p. ED 092 301
  Books of fiction and non-fiction for junior high and
high school on the above topics. Arranged by citations listed
alphabetically by author under each minority group.
  This bibliography has 67 descriptively annotated citations on Mexican Americans. It is a multidisciplinary list
that has poetry, novels, political science and studies on discrimination. The compiler has presented a good cross section limiting herself mainly to Mexican Americans. She also
indicates where book was reviewed. Unfortunately she has
left off some very basic works, e.g. , Tomas Rivera's ...
And the Earth Did Not Part and Rudy Anaya's Bless Me Ultima, both Quinto Sol winners.

2 Alternative Press Index; An Index to the Publications which
Amplify the Cry for Social Change and Social Justice,
1969 to 1971. Toronto: Radical Research Center.
  An index "to provide access to the mountain of facts,
thoughts and theories which are being turned out by the revolutionary movement of this country and the world." Index to
current periodicals that would not normally be included in
standard indexes. Does index some old magazines but emphasis on new underground magazines and newspapers. Arranged
alphabetically by subject. Articles arranged chronologically
by magazine issue date.
  Includes many subjects other than Chicanos. However,
its value as a Mexican-American reference tool is its inclusion of articles from periodicals that would not be listed in
standard indexes. Has section on Chicanos and also cross
references. For example, issue no. 1 has over 50 references
to Mexican Americans. Unfortunately latest issue so far
(1974) is dated 1971. Number of issues per year varies.

1

3   Altus, David M. Bilingual Education: A Selected Bibli-
     ography. Las Cruces, N. M.: Educational Resource
     Information Center, n. d. 222p.
          "Provide[s] access to some of the latest findings and
developments in the areas of bilingualism and bilingual education. " Contains books and articles from Research in Education and Current Index to Journals in Education. Divided
into two parts, i. e. , each one devoted to one of the above
mentioned sources. Subject index based upon the ERIC
Thesaurus.
          204 entries each with accession number, clearinghouse
accession number, publication date, title, author, summary
and journal citation. Excellent summaries of many of the
articles; 42 entries specifically on Mexican Americans and
naturally many others relevant to this subject.

4   Alvarez, Grace de Jesús C. Topónimos en Apellidos His-
     panos. Garden City, N. Y.: Adelphi University, 1968.
     584p.
          An attempt to trace the origin of Spanish surnames
found in the 1960 Madrid telephone directory. Analysis of
Madrileño names only. In addition to the name dictionary,
the author also devotes the three initial chapters to a study
of surnames in Spain. Alphabetical by surname. Also lists
40 pages of names from the Madrid phone directory that do
not have a geographical origin.
          Lists approximately 3164 Spanish surnames. Each
entry has origin, discussion of origin by experts, also geographical source when possible. Author divides personal
names into three large groups: personal that are derived
from an adjective or name a profession; patronymic or those
names that derive from a Christian name; and finally names
taken from the geographical location of the originator of the
family. Though peninsular in origin, this work obviously
contains many Mexican American family names and is excellent for identity with Hispanic heritage.

5   American Council on Race Relations. Mexican Americans:
     A Selected Bibliography. Chicago: American Coun-
     cil on Race Relations, 1949. (Bibliographic Series,
     no. 7.)
          A guide to print materials on Mexican Americans:
bibliographies, books, pamphlets, reprints, and periodicals.
Mainly 1930 to ca. 1949 and arranged in this order.
          Not many Mexican-American bibliographies predate

this one. It is an early attempt to list works on this ethnic group long before a recognizable Chicano movement had begun. Contains 105 unannotated entries. The citations are mainly on works in history and social sciences. Periodicals here refer to articles. Surely all of these entries have now been absorbed by more recent and more inclusive bibliographies; however, it is good as an early effort at Chicano bibliography.

6   American Library Association. Adult Services Division.
    Subcommittee on Spanish Materials. Films for Spanish-Speaking and Spanish Culture Groups. n. p. [1971?]
    16p.
    Guide to 60 films and filmstrips that date from 1937 to 1971 for adult groups, with an orientation towards Mexican, Puerto Rican and Spanish themes or universal themes such as birth. Arranged alphabetically by title. Divided into films and filmstrips. Final page has list of distributors.
    Of the 60 titles, approximately seven are strictly pertinent to Mexican Americans. The others pertain to other Hispanic cultures or are multicultural. Each entry has title, language, length, color, date, and producer. Also a brief descriptive paragraph on content. Probably Cynthia Baird's La Raza in Films would be a necessary supplement. Films for Spanish Speaking might be useful for teachers of beginners in this language.

7   American Library Association. Adult Services Division.
    Subcommittee on Spanish Materials. Suppliers of Spanish-Language Materials. n. p. , n. d. , 6p.
    Guide to approximately 60 sources of Spanish materials in the U. S. , Mexico, Argentina and Spain arranged alphabetically by publisher.
    Each entry with address and short descriptive paragraph of type of catalogs available from each source. Materials are Spanish and not specifically Mexican American. Would be invaluable for teachers of Mexican Americans who want various types of reading materials in Spanish.

8   Atienza, Julio de. Diccionario nobilario. Madrid: Aguilar, 1959. 1084p.
    This work in Spanish is mainly a guide to the noble families of Spain but also has supplementary material on heraldry and titles. Its scope is enormous, as suggested by

the total number of pages. Apparently the user can find
not only the family but also some explanation of heraldry
and titles. Atienza divides this work into three distinct
sections: I Nociones de heráldica; II Diccionario heráldico
de apellidos; and III Diccionario de títulos nobilarios. The
appendix contains supplementary information on noble titles.
The alphabetical arrangement of names facilitates use. The
major value of Atienza's work is the second and third sections. For here are approximately 17,478 names each with
varying information: geographical origin of family, the dif-
fusion of the family through Spain and at times the Americas,
the first member of the family to be included in the nobility,
the meretorious deed worthy of nobility, and a description of
the coat of arms. This is by no means a personal name dictionary, but it does serve the purpose of identity since the
Mexican American can often find his own name among the
17,478. This does not indicate noble descent, but probably
at the most means that certain people with the same name
have titles and coats of arms. The value of Atienza is as
another source for surname identification. It is supplemental
to Alvarez' Topónimos en Apellidos Hispanos in 1968 and
Tibón's Onomástica hispanoamericana.

9   Austin, Texas. Public Works. Records of Austin Cem-
      eteries [computer printout]. Austin [1974?].
         Lists all of the recorded burials in the cemeteries of
Austin, Texas: Oakwood, Evergreen, Memorial, Mt. Calvary,
Bethany, Travis County International, State Plummer, etc.
From 1854 to present. Arranged alphabetically by surname.
All cemeteries integrated into one list.
         This is a computer printout updated periodically. Ap-
proximately 50,000 entries with date buried, name, cemetery,
section lot and space. Most of the names are Anglo but in-
numerable Spanish surnames, e.g., 139 Martinez's listed.
Valuable source for genealogical work among Mexican Americans.

10   Baird, Cynthia. La Raza in Films: A List of Films and
       Filmstrips. Oakland, Cal.: Latin American Library,
       197? 68p.
         An annotated guide to films and filmstrips about Mexi-
can Americans and Latin Americans. (Raza here refers to
Mexican American and all other Latin Americans.) Divided
into four parts: I. Background on Mexico and Latin America;
II. The Spanish-speaking in the U.S.; III. The Third World

and Latin America; and IV. Directory of Film Producers and
Distributors.
    Part II lists 63 16mm. films which pertain to Mexi-
can Americans. The variety runs from harmless cultural
films to those of extreme militancy. Each entry includes
length, language, price, distributor, and a descriptive annotation.

11 Baird, Cynthia (comp.). Supplement to La Raza in
    Films. Oakland, Cal. : Latin American Library of
    the Oakland Public Library, 1974. 6p.
    (See the above entry.) Covers 1972 to 1974. Back-
ground on Mexico and Latin America, the Spanish-speaking
in the U. S. , the Third World in Latin America, and directory of film producers and distributors, arranged in that
order. All films are listed in the table of contents.
    This supplements the 1972 edition by adding 19 new
titles. Each is annotated with a descriptive paragraph. In
addition are given color, length, language, price and distributor. At least six of the films deal with the Mexican
Americans, while the others are mainly Latin American and
relate to social protest. This is one of the few separate
film bibliographies, since most are incorporated within monographs.

12 Baird, Newton D. , and Robert Greenwood. An Anno-
    tated Bibliography of California Fiction. Georgetown,
    Cal. : Talisman Literary Research, Inc. , 1971. 521p.
    Bibliography of novels and short stories written about
California; i.e. , locale is the main criterion. Mainly 20th
but also 19th century. All entries alphabetized by author surname. Two excellent indexes--locale and subject.
    2, 711 annotated entries, each with author, title, pub-
lisher, date, pages, one-sentence summary, and sources of
information. 26 entries on Mexican Americans and related
references under peripheral subjects such as Mexican California, Mexicans, migrants, Spanish California, etc. One of
the few annotated bibliographies on Mexican Americans in fiction. Earliest entries about 1900 and latest about 1970.

13 Banco de México. Biblioteca. Bibliografía sobre migra-
    ción de trabajadores mexicanos a los Estados Unidos
    [mimeographed]. Mexico City: Banco de México,
    1959. 122p.

Notes publications on this topic solely from the point
of view of the U.S.   Covers years 1950 to 1958.   Mainly
journal and newspaper articles but also some books.   All
aspects of the subject.   Divided into four main sections--
government documents, magazine articles, books, and New
York Times articles.   No index.
The compiler relied on 11 catalogues and indexes in
order to complete this bibliography.   No annotations except
articles from New York Times are summarized as in the
New York Times Index.   No theses or dissertations used.

14   Banks, Vera J., Elsie S. Manny, and Nelson L. LeRay.
Research Data on Minority Groups: An Annotated Bibliography of Economic Research Service Reports:
1955-1965.   Washington, D.C.: U.S. Dept. of Agriculture, 1966.   25p.
"... a guide to information on minority groups published by the Economic Research Service and its predecessor
agencies." U.S. in general and specifically 12 states that
have minority groups in agriculture.   All print materials.
Arranged U.S. in general, then the entries listed alphabetically under the 12 individual states.   Table of contents.   Author
index and subject index.
76 annotated entries and 16 unannotated.   Nine of these
annotated entries refer specifically to Spanish Americans and
others are probably subsumed under other titles although not
mentioned.   Three states listed are California, New Mexico
and Texas.   Themes vary--economic, demographic, bracero,
technological, etc.   Very good descriptive annotations.   One
of few bibliographies of government documents on Mexican
Americans.   One wonders why Arizona and Colorado were
excluded.

15   Barnes, Regina.   A Selected ERIC Bibliography on Teaching Ethnic Minority Group Children in the United
States of America.   New York: Columbia University,
Teachers College, ERIC Information Retrieval Center
on the Disadvantaged, 1969.   22p.
Provides helpful information on ERIC materials for
those who work with the children of ethnic minority groups.
A general bibliography on teaching ethnic minorities comes
first; then four sections on special minority groups, including
the Mexican American.
In the two sections pertinent to the Mexican American
are 14 well-annotated entries.   These have the usual ERIC

format which provides an abstract more than an annotation.
Probably the most helpful are the selections on teaching ethnic minorities in general, for here are works often overlooked in the more traditional bibliographies. Unfortunately,
limiting entries to ERIC materials prohibits the inclusion of
some basic bibliographies on children's literature.

16 Barnes, William C. Arizona Place Names. Tucson:
     University of Arizona Press, 1960. 519p.
     Guide to place names of Arizona for which information
is available. Covers entire state and includes pronunciation,
elevation, historical sketch, and further references. Arranged alphabetically by county. An index leads to the county
then the place name is located alphabetically under this.
Cross references also available.
     Spanish and Indian place names are integrated with
Anglo names. Includes innumerable Spanish place names and
when possible gives information about the origin and a few
historical facts.

17 Barrios, Ernie. Bibliografía de Aztlán: An Annotated
     Chicano Bibliography. San Diego, Cal.: Centro de
     Estudios Chicanos, 1971. 145p.
     Attempts to cover all areas of Chicanismo in print.
Divided into 13 sections, including pre-Columbian history to
the present. Divided into overlapping categories, e.g., contemporary history, high school materials, native Americans.
Author and title index but no topical index.
     Barrios has a great consciousness for la raza and
feels that much literature written about the Chicano is "...
biased and has perpetuated long standing negative stereotypes
...." Therefore with each entry he gives a long annotation
or rather abstract describing the contents and noting the author's biases. These are often good critical annotations.
This is the main value of his bibliography. The selections
are on Mexico, the Mexican American and works of a general nature. Some of the entries seem too peripheral, e.g.,
Vine Deloria's Custer Died for Your Sins. Conversely he
leaves out John Steinbeck and Willa Cather who do relate directly to the Chicanos. One integrated list and an excellent
subject index would have eliminated the need for multiple
categories.

18 Belden Associates. The Mexican-American Market in

the United States.   Dallas: Belden Associates, 1962.
39p.
Intended "To meet the need for reliable marketing data
on the Spanish-language, Mexican American population of the
U. S. " Covers urban Arizona, California, Colorado, New
Mexico, and Texas.   Apparently, figures gathered in early
1960's.   Market characteristics and city and county populations.   Two sections--market characteristics and cities and
county populations.   Detailed table of contents but no index.
Study somewhat dated now but contains valuable information on Mexican Americans, e. g. , standard of living as
suggested by t. v. ownership, family income, home ownership.
Also cultural level, e. g. , language preference, newspaper and
magazine reading, movie-going, education of head of family,
etc.   Second part contains a breakdown of Mexican-American
population by city and county.   Census data derived from 500
interviews proportioned according to density of distribution of
Mexican Americans.

19   Bengelsdorf, Winnie.   Ethnic Studies in Higher Education:
     State of the Art and Bibliography.   Washington, D. C. :
     American Assoc. of State Colleges and Universities,
     1972.   260p.
Attempts to identify and summarize materials on ethnic studies at the college level.   Has chapter on state of the
art of ethnic studies plus chapters on each numerically important ethnic group in the U. S. --i. e. , Chicanos, Blacks,
Asians, Indians, etc.   Arranged with general chapters pertinent to all ethnic groups.   Also has the individual chapters
mentioned above.   Author and title index.
Only a part of this work is valuable for the Chicano.
The section on Chicano studies is comprised of entries on
surveys and research, pending research, history and sociological sources, periodicals, bibliography and institutions offering Chicano studies.   The introductory chapter on state of
the art gives a general view of ethnic studies in the United
States.

20   Benitez, Frank, and Sharon Benitez.   Practical Spanish
     for the Health Professions.   Fresno, Cal. : Pioneer
     Pub. Co. , 1973.   305p.
Designed to help give better health care to the 13
million people in the U. S. who speak only Spanish by providing simple but standard Spanish for the non-Hispanic.   Bilingual sentences relating to health and health care.   Divided

into three major sections--general medicine, specialized medicine and mental health. Detailed table of contents but no index of medical terms.
Valuable for its bilingual sentences on health problems. Presupposes certain linguistic sophistication of user in order to understand and repeat the Spanish translations. Lacking is a glossary of basic medical terms and an index to lead the reader to the proper term. Work is good as is but glossary and index would have made it excellent.

21 Birdwell, Gladys Bryant, and Perry Garner Little.
    Chicanos: A Selected Bibliography. Houston, Texas: University of Houston Libraries, 1971. 60p.
    A guide to Chicano material in the University of Houston Library. Books, government documents, and articles. Materials on immigration, Mexico and Mexican Americans. Arranged by format. No index. Approximately 325 unannotated entries.
    Although title states, "A Selected Bibliography," no introduction or preface gives criteria of selection. In other words, why the presence of an occasional title on Texas and the innumerable ones on Mexico? For more recent holdings at the University of Houston, see entry under University of Houston.

22 Bischof, Phyllis. Ethnic Studies: A Selective Guide to Reference Materials at Berkeley. Berkeley: University of California General Library, 1974. (Occasional Publications, no. 1.) 52p.
    "... A selective, annotated guide to those bibliographies, abstracts, indexes, and other reference works judged to be most useful in the exploration of ethnic studies materials...." Card catalogs, description of library units (i. e. , reference service, documents, etc.), guides to periodical literature and abstracts, and bibliographies. Covers various ethnic groups including the Chicano. Author and title indexes.
    This appears to be a guide done by an experienced reference librarian who understands user needs. Two sections of value for Mexican American studies--guides to periodical literature and abstracts and the Chicano section of bibliographies. The former lists and annotates 22 guides and abstracts that would contain the latest materials on Mexican Americans. The latter lists 26 annotated bibliographies on all aspects of Chicanismo. This is one of the few bibliographies done by a reference expert and for that reason the ma-

terial is invaluable.   Most bibliographies overlook the guides
to periodicals.

23   Blanco S., Antonio.   La lengua española en la historia
     de California: contribución a su estudio.   Madrid:
     Ediciones Cultura Hispánica, 1971.   827p.
     Traces the evolution of the Spanish language within the
history of California from the beginnings of the Hispanic period to the present.   Both history and philology.   Composed
of five separate dictionaries plus chapters on histories and
introductory section to each dictionary.
     Must be one of the main sources on California Spanish.
The five dictionaries are: vocabulario de californianismos,
the Gold Rush and the Spanish speaking, Spanish influence on
English, Spanish terms in English, and new words and pachu-
quismos.   This is an excellent study.   Is well annotated, has
methodological chapter, and a 20-page bibliography.

24   Bloom, Lansing B. (ed.).   New Mexico Historical Re-
     view.   1926- .   Quarterly.   Comprehensive Index to
     Volumes I-XV, 1926-1940; Frank D. Reeves, Compre-
     hensive Index to Volumes XVI-XXX, 1941-1955; Kath-
     erine McMahon, Comprehensive Index ... 1956-70.
     Each volume of this index provides a cumulative index
for every 15 years of issues of the New Mexico Historical
Review, a publication that concentrates mainly on the history
of New Mexico.   The three indexes cover approximately 45
years of this quarterly.   Each of the three parts of the index
contains the table of contents for all of the volumes incorporated within the 15-year time period.   Each also has a
single integrated index of authors, titles of articles, titles of
books reviewed, and subjects.
     Index to approximately 135 articles and innumerable
book reviews.   The Mexican American not singled out as a
subject but surely incorporated in many of the articles.
Much on the colonial period of New Mexico and also the 19th
century.   Easy to locate topics now because of excellent indexing.   Probably one of best historical sources on Hispanos
of New Mexico.

25   Bogardus, Emory S.   The Mexican Immigrant: An Anno-
     tated Bibliography.   Los Angeles: The Council on In-
     ternational Relations, 1929.   21p.
     An overview of the Mexican immigrant starting with

his native culture, continuing with studies in the U.S., and
ending with interracial adjustments.   Articlés and books
mainly dating from the 20th century.   Divided into three parts
--culture backgrounds, studies in the United States, and interracial adjustments.   Each of the three sections separated into books and articles.
      Approximately 200 annotated entries.   This must be
one of the first bibliographies on the topic of Mexican Americans and consequently could be considered a primitive index
of the status of Mexican American studies at that time.
Largest section is on studies in the United States.   See Robert C. Jones.

26   Bolton, Herbert F.   Guide to Materials for the History
      of the United States in the Principal Archives of Mex-
      ico.   Washington, D.C.:   Carnegie Institute, 1913.
      553p.
      Intended to encourage and assist Americans to use the
Mexican archives.   Inventories 15 archives within Mexico
City and also the various archives in 17 states and cities
throughout the republic.   Most materials are for the 18th and
19th centuries.   Has excellent table of contents and 72-page
name and place index.
      This work definitely relates to Mexican Americans be-
cause it has numerous entries under the states that once belonged to Mexico.   Bolton explains origin of collection for
each archive, its relationship to United States history, and
the types of materials found within.   Each entry, usually explained in English, is labeled by volume number and brief
description.

27   Bowen, Jean Donald.   The Spanish of San Antonito, New
      Mexico.   Ph.D. dissertation.   Albuquerque: Univer-
      sity of New Mexico, 1952.   373p.
      A description of the phonology and morphology of the
language of San Antonito.   Its main aim is to provide a description of a spoken Spanish dialect.   Phonology, phonemes,
allophone distribution, intonemes, English borrowings, morphology, vocabulary, etc., arranged in this order.
      The main section of this dissertation is the dictionary
of words from San Antonito.   It comprises 197 pages or almost 4000 words.   Although the author cautions that this is
not complete enough to be called a "dictionary," it may be
used as such.   For it contains entries that "range from
archaisms to the latest pachuco slang."   Each entry with

phonetic transcriptions, gender indication, and meaning. Often the full and reduced forms are entered for one word. No etymology or use in context. Although almost half of this study is devoted to pronunciation and other aspects of the language, the most valuable section for the Mexican Americanist is probably vocabulary. It may serve as a primitive dictionary.

28 Boyd-Bowman, Peter. Indice geobiográfico de cuarenta mil pobladores españoles de América en el siglo XVI. Vol. I, 1493-1519; vol. II, 1520-1539. Bogotá: Instituto Caro y Cuervo, 1964; Mexico City: Editorial Jus, 1968.

Guide to 40,000 Spaniards who immigrated to the Americas in the 16th century. Family and given names of immigrants, relationship, profession and social status, and region of origin in Spain. From 1493 to 1539. Organized alphabetically by regions in Spain and then surnames entered under region. Indexes of surnames, professional and social status, index of destination and places in America, and expeditions.

Excellent reference for Mexican American with genealogical or historical interests. Many of the emigrants came to New Spain. Highly compact information in two volumes. Thorough indexing. Extensive bibliography. Also maps and charts indicating origins, years and percentages of immigrants. These two volumes appear to be the results of a very meticulous investigation into various sources.

29 Brown, Mary J. Handy Index to the Holdings of the Genealogical Society of Utah. Logan, Utah: Everton Publishers, 1971. 150p.

A guide to the branch libraries of this society and also a bibliography of the genealogical information available in each of the 50 states and Federal District. States are divided into two separate sections, general information and county information. The former briefly lists various types of records for each state: church, emigration, census, land and property, military, vital, probate, and miscellaneous. County information refers to: cemeteries, lawsuits, marriages, civil records, deeds, etc.

This section on states and counties comprises the major portion of the index. Of similar value are the five pages of addresses of branch libraries of the Genealogical Society given by state; 35 of these libraries serve Arizona, California, Colorado, New Mexico and Texas. Throughout the United

States the (Mormon) Church of Jesus Christ of Latter Day
Saints has established a network for genealogical information.
Each branch library has a microfilm of the main card cata-
logue of the Genealogical Society of Utah. Users, through
the services of the branch libraries, may borrow any micro-
film from the main library in Utah. In other words, Handy
Index is indispensable for beginning research on Mexican-
American families.

30 Browning, Harvey L., and S. Dale McLemore. Statis-
    tical Profile of the Spanish-Surname Population of
    Texas. Austin: University of Texas Bureau of Busi-
    ness Research, 1964. 83p. (Population Series, No.
    1.)
        Presents the basic characteristics of the Chicano pop-
ulation in Texas from 1950 to 1960. Includes numbers, geographical distribution, education, employment, and interstate
comparisons, in that order. Information is set out mainly
in 33 tables. No index.
        Highly compressed survey of Texan Chicanos. Tables
on multiple aspects of this ethnic group: income, occupational categories, residence, school enrollment, family, etc.

31 Butte County [Cal.] Superintendent of Schools. Ethnic
    and Cultural Bibliography; Africa and the Negroes,
    American Indians, Asiatic Americans, Spanish Speak-
    ing Americans. Oroville, Cal.: Butte County Super-
    intendent of Schools, 1970. 53p.
        Lists monographs published since 1930 for primary,
intermediate, and advanced classes on the four ethnic groups
mentioned in the title, divided according to ethnic groups,
and then by age levels.
        Only the final section is devoted to Spanish-speaking
Americans. Has approximately 153 annotated titles mainly
fiction. About one-third of these are in Spanish. This bibliography is ideal for the school with students from several
different ethnic minorities; however, southwestern schools
would probably prefer a bibliography that deals mainly with
Mexican Americans and that has multi-media. For this purpose Margaret S. Nichols' works (q.q.v.) are superior.

32 Butterfield, Mary. A Bibliography and Guide to Chicano
    Materials in the Eastern Michigan University Library.
    Ypsilanti: Eastern Michigan University Library, 1972.

19p.

A guide on how to do research in Chicano studies in the EMU Library and an annotated listing of a cross section of materials in this field--monographs, periodical articles, pamphlets, and documents, on social science, history and education. Integrated list alphabetized by author surname. Subject index.

116 annotated entries from the various contributing disciplines on Chicanismo. Superior to most bibliographies because of the annotations, the subject index, the cross section of materials, the three-page guide on how to do research on Chicanos, and the exclusion of most materials from Mexico. However, Juan Rulfo's The Burning Plain and Other Stories seems anomalous in this bibliography.

33 Caballero, César, and Ken Hedman. Chicano Studies
     Bibliography. El Paso: University of Texas at El
     Paso, 1973. 53p.

Guide to Chicano materials at the UTEP library. 453 books and periodical articles, magazines and audio visual materials. Part I is on books and magazine articles entered by author surname when possible. Part II is an alphabetical list of magazines then newspapers and Part III, audiovisual materials. Subject index and co-author index.

One of the better bibliographies for one institution's holdings on Chicanos. Many of the entries are annotated. In addition to traditional Chicano materials, this bibliography also lists related works on Mexico and sociological studies relevant to the Chicago.

34 Cabaza, Berta. The Spanish Language in Texas. No.
     2. Cameron and Willacy Counties. Master's thesis,
     University of Texas at Austin, 1950. 183p.

To note the peculiarities of the Spanish language in these two Texan counties. Vocabulary and idiomatic phrases of the Spanish-speaking; and hispanismos used by the English-speaking of the same area.

The author's criterion for the regional Spanish of these south Texas counties is that the word not be listed in the 1947 edition of the Diccionario de la Academia Española or be listed with a different meaning. Approximately 900 entries each with gender, regional definition and contrasting definition from the area. Also includes 400 idiomatic phrases and proverbs. All in Spanish.

on Mexican Americans   15

35 California. Department of Education. Racial and Ethnic
    Survey of California Public Schools. Sacramento:
    GPO [1968?]. 80?p.
    This is an attempt to determine progress "in securing
an equitable distribution of members of all racial and ethnic
groups in school systems throughout the state." Survey was
made during 1967 and 1968. Schools here refer mainly to
kindergarten through college, but emphasis is at the lower
levels. In addition to Spanish surname, Negro and Orientals
also included. Arranged in two parts: distribution of pupils
and distribution of employees. Gives an excellent introduction
on procedures and methods of selection.
    Main value in the first study is the collection of 19
tables dealing with a diversity of topics relating to ethnic distribution. Part II has text and tables relating to ethnic employees in the California school system. Data no longer current but have value as a guideline in judging integration of a
state school program. Copy obtained from state library in
Sacramento, Calif.

36 California. Department of Industrial Relations. Division
    of Labor Statistics and Research. Californians of
    Spanish Surname. San Francisco, n.p., 1964. 54p.
    Concise presentation of sociological factors relevant
to the Mexican American in California from 1950 to 1960.
Population; education and size of family; labor force, employment and unemployment; income, in that order. No index
but detailed list of tables and charts.
    Very compact study of Mexican American that is some-
what dated now; 23 tables refine the general subject headings
listed above.

37 California. Office of the Surveyor General. Corrected
    Report of Spanish and Mexican Grants in California
    Complete to February 25, 1886. Published as Supple-
    ment to Official Report of 1883-84 [microfilm]. Sac-
    ramento, 1886. 19p.
    Guide to grants of land in California made by Spanish
or Mexican authorities to 1886 as suggested in title. Lists
approximately 595 grants. Entered alphabetically by name of
grant. Basic information for grants: number on map, name
of grant, confirmee, size of area, condition of title, and
where located.
    This reference of interest to Mexican Americans: it
is a primitive type of geographical dictionary to California for

the names of the grant and the areas where grant was located.
Almost half of the confirmees are of Spanish surname. For
genealogical studies, land grants are often one of the best
sources for 19th-century United States. This is a document
that confirms the Hispanic roots of California. Obtained from
Library of Congress.

38 California Pioneer Register and Index, 1542-1848. In-
    cluding Inhabitants of California, 1796-1800 and List
    of Pioneers Extracted from the History of California
    by Hubert Howe Bancroft. Baltimore: Regional Pub.
    Co., 1964. 392p.
    Includes in one volume all of the genealogical informa-
tion from Bancroft's seven-volume History of California.
Original author included all names of prominence he could
find in archives, public, private and missional; personal
reminiscences, and the works of specialists. Arranged alphabetically and chronologically into four periods according
to when the person's name first appeared in the sources.
    1680 Mexican Americans are listed and approximately
150 Anglos. Each entry includes: date name encountered,
residence, brief history, death, name of spouse, and citation
where found in Bancroft's History of California.

39 California Polytechnic State University. San Luis Obispo
    Library. Afro-American and Mexican American Bib-
    liography. San Luis Obispo, 1969. 155p.
    Preliminary listing of materials relating to Afro-Amer-
icans and Mexican Americans in Library of California Polytechnic State University. Mainly monographs, government
publications and periodicals. Also study kits, filmstrips and
transparencies. Arranged by location of materials in the library; i.e., books from the general collection, curriculum
library materials, government publications and periodicals.
Blacks and Mexican Americans entered under these headings.
No index or refined table of contents.
    This bibliography is extremely difficult to use. Eith-
er the two minority groups should have separate bibliographies
or this one should be well indexed. Mainly materials on
Blacks; however, Chicanos are entered under: Mexican Americans in the U.S., Minorities in the Rocky Mountains and
Southwest, and Economic history and conditions. At times
the two ethnic groups are listed separately; on occasion they
are integrated into one list. In other words, the user is
forced to peruse much extraneous material to find the sought
after entry. No annotations.

40 California State College, Los Angeles. John F. Kennedy
Memorial Library. A Library Guide to Mexican American Studies. Los Angeles: California State College,
n. d. 14p.
Bibliography of books in this library for the study of
the Mexican American. Covers bibliographies, periodicals
and newspapers, books, current abstracts and master's
theses, in that order. No articles or non-print materials.
Too brief to require an index.
94 entries, many annotated. A problem is the lack
of an introduction to note criteria and limitations. This bibliography has much emphasis on Mexico and Latin America,
but its main contribution is in the initial pages which instruct
the user in search strategies for materials on the Mexican
American. Most useful (and almost invariably lacking in all
other bibliographies) is the list of subject headings used in
the card catalog for related materials on the Mexican American.

41 California State College, Sonoma. Chicano Studies De-
partment. Chicano Children's Literature; Annotated
Bibliography Compiled by Mexican American Children's
Librarians in Fall, 1972. Sonoma: California State
College, 1972. 39p.
A guide to books with a Chicano theme published between 1950 and 1970 for grades k-12, mainly 1-6. Mostly
English but some Spanish, in both fiction and non-fiction.
Alphabetized by author. No index or cross references.
Approximately 230 titles listed. Each with bibliographical information, a synopsis, appropriate age group, and a
number indicating the evaluator's rating. Judgment for this
rating was based on: (1) characters should seem real; (2)
attitude should be one we want people to have without over-
doing the dialect; (3) a modern story should not have nos-
talgia for the past; (4) illustrations should be kindly; (5) the
book should have literary merit. Although these criteria
might be faulty or subjective, they do give one judgment of
a book. Excellent for grade school teachers and librarians.

42 California State Library, Sacramento. A Quarterly Bibliography on Cultural Differences. 1964-
A periodical guide to monographs, government documents and articles on the cultural minorities in the U. S. including the Mexican American. Mainly current materials in
social sciences, education, and history. Each quarterly issue

has approximately 50 entries listed alphabetically by author.
Later issues use ethnic groups as topical subdivisions.
        This is an on-going publication sponsored by the State
Library of California.   Each issue has basic bibliographic
information plus descriptive annotations that vary from a few
lines to 100 words.   As an example of its scope, one issue
listed articles from 26 different periodicals.   Many relatively
unknown.   "Cultural difference" can be interpreted broadly to
mean any ethnic minority in the U.S. --e.g., Norwegians.
Most entries are on Blacks, but many also on Mexican Americans.   The latter form only a small portion of each issue,
but this publication is useful because of its currency.   Also
has many entries on prejudice and cultural differences in
general.

43   California State University, Fresno.   The Library.
        Afro- and Mexican-Americans; Books and Other Ma-
        terials in the Library of Fresno State College Relat-
        ing to the History, Culture, and Problems of Afro-
        Americans and Mexican-Americans.   Fresno, 1969.
        109p.
        A guide to all topics on the two ethnic groups in books,
government publications and master's theses in the Fresno
State College Library.   Although periodicals of Black and
Chicanos are mentioned, no reference is made to specific
articles.   Arranged by format--i.e., books in numerical order according to L.C. classification, then government publications in alphabetical order, and then theses in alphabetical order by author.   No index.
        Over 75 percent of the bibliography is devoted to Black
materials.   Black and Mexican-American materials are not
separated in this bibliography.   No annotations and the lack
of an index make this difficult to use.

44   California State University, Hayward.   Library.   Chicano
        Bibliography.   Hayward, 1970.   70p.
        A comprehensive listing of library sources, mainly
monographs, on Mexican Americans, Mexican culture, and
California and Southwestern history.   Arranged by topic: history of Mexico and U.S. relations, Mexican cultural and ethnic heritage of Chicanos, the Mexican becomes Mexican American, the Chicano in the U.S., aspects of Chicano life, Chicano culture, biography, juvenile books, newspapers and periodicals, and bibliographies.   Has table of contents and author
index only.

    This bibliography has potential, for the compilers at
least attempted to establish guidelines in regard to Mexico,
but admit to the arbitrariness of the selection.   500 unannotated entries compose this work.   Although it presents a
good cross section, it does have several problems.   The
subject divisions are too overlapping and could have been
handled in a subject index.   No periodical articles are mentioned.   Of value is the seven-page orientation on the use of
the library.

45   California State University, Long Beach.   Library.   Chi-
      cano Bibliography: A Selected List of Books on the
      Culture, History, and Socio-Economic Conditions of
      the Mexican American.   Long Beach, 1970.   45p.
      Designed to aid those seeking to identify with and un-
derstand the Chicanos.   Very broad scope including books
(only) on Mexico and much of southwestern history and culture, divided into 23 subject divisions.   Entries are not
alphabetized and there is no index.
    The scope of this bibliography is practically unlimited;
in addition to Chicanos and Mexicans, it also incorporates
Central America, Indians of North America, U.S. political
history, etc.   Too many topics actually peripheral to the
Chicano.   Lack of index and alphabetization makes use difficult.

46   Campa, Arthur L.   A Bibliography of Spanish Folklore
      in New Mexico.   Albuquerque: University of New
      Mexico, 1930.   28p.   (University of New Mexico Bul-
      letin-Language series, vol. 2, no. 3.)
      Catalogs materials on Hispanic folklore from southern
Colorado and northern New Mexico, mainly songs and poetry
of the above mentioned area.   Divided according to form:
Décima, indita, cuando, romance, corrido, folksong, alabado,
verso popular, riddles and sayings, religious drama, secular
drama, and folktales.   No index or table of contents but the
work is brief.
    Very early attempt to collect Hispanic folklore in New
Mexico and Colorado.   Each section composed of two parts--
definition and then list of examples.   It is to be hoped that the
lists have been updated with more recent research.   As it stands,
this bibliography is highly informative to the amateur folklorist
because it suggests the variety of oral folklore.   The expert
would perhaps prefer the full text of the titles.   This work
hints at the potential for study in the field of oral folklore.

47 Cárdenas, Gilbert. Selected Bibliography Pertaining to:
    La Raza in the Midwest and Great Lakes States, 1924-
    1973. Notre Dame, Ind. : Centro de Estudios e In-
    vestigaciones Sociales, 1973.
        A guide to all Hispanic print materials--journal arti-
    cles, position papers, monographs, dissertations, state and
    government documents, newspapers, magazines and periodi-
    cals--in the Great Lakes states. Mainly social science;
    1924-1973. All the above are integrated into one sequence
    arranged alphabetically by author except serials, which are
    listed separately.
        Of all of the bibliographies listed in the present work,
    this is the only one that pertains to the Mexican American in
    the Great Lakes states. Approximately 240 unannotated en-
    tries. This bibliography has a very definite social science
    emphasis and does not list creative works of a literary nature
    or non-print materials. Mexican Americans occasionally
    identified in the title. Valuable for its regional emphasis.

48 Cartel: Annotated Bibliography of Bilingual Bicultural
    Materials No. 12 Cumulative Issue--1973. Austin,
    Texas: Education Service Center 13. ED 806 429
        A guide to multiethnic materials both print and non-
    print at the Education Service Center in Austin. Has materi-
    als on Mexico, the Mexican American, French, Puerto Rican,
    American Indian, etc. However, the Mexican American pre-
    dominates. Seems mainly for elementary level. Entries are
    in one list entered alphabetically by title. Has title index
    and index to titles of materials in series.
        Approximately 90 well-annotated entries. Each with
    complete bibliographical information, and a long descriptive
    paragraph often giving not only contents but suggested age
    level and value of work. Excellent guide with much useful
    material for teacher in the Southwest. Multiple aspects of
    the Mexican American covered: language, life in the barrio,
    Mexican-American values, etc.

49 Caselli, Ron, and the Sonoma County [Cal.] Ethnic Studies
    Curriculum Committee. The Minority Experience: A
    Basic Bibliography of American Ethnic Studies. Santa
    Rosa, Cal. : Sonoma County Office of Education.
    n. d.   73p.
        Intended to "afford teachers a good, general background
    on American minority groups." Monographs on Afro-, Mexi-
    can and Native Americans, arranged in this order. Alpha-

betical by author.   No index.
Approximately 225 unannotated entries on the Mexican
American.   This is a basic bibliography mainly for high
school and junior high school teachers, students and librarians.   Consequently, representative works from all disciplines relating to Mexican Americans.   Also lists some of
the standard works from Mexico.   Leaves out American creative fiction such as Steinbeck and Willa Cather.   Missing
also are some basic bibliographies.

50   Caskey, Owen L., and Jimmy Hodges.   A Resource and
     Reference Bibliography on Teaching and Counseling the
     Bilingual Student.   Lubbock, Texas: School of Educa-
     tion, 1968.   45p.
A review of pertinent literature in the field of teaching and counseling bilingual students, including monographs
and articles from about 1921 to 1967.   Much on Mexican
Americans and Indian Americans but other minorities also
mentioned.   A study of the titles incorporated suggests that
all aspects of education are included.   Completely integrated
list with no subtopics, alphabetized by author surname.   No
index.
733 unannotated entries.   Although the compilers feel
that each user might want to scan the entire list to find what
is relevant, thus obviating the need for subtopics, a subject
index would have aided greatly.   Nor do the authors list
sources for information.   Wide variety of journals used,
some dissertations and government documents.   The guidelines for this bibliography were extremely broad in scope in
that the compilers have included much that is peripheral but
useful, e.g., Cather's Death Comes for the Archbishop.
Caskey and Hodges have the opinion that an article pertinent
to one minority group will have parallels for another minority
group.   This bibliography now needs updating, but is still
highly useful.

51   Castañeda, Carlos Eduardo.   Catálogo de manuscritos
     para la historia de Texas y Provincias Internas en el
     archivo del antiguo convento de San Francisco el
     Grande de México [typescript].   Austin: University of
     Texas, n.d.   13p.
As title indicates, guide to manuscripts in the San
Francisco Convent in Mexico.   Most of the items relate to
provinces other than Texas.   However, many do relate to
Texas.   1673 to 1792.   Itemizes legajos 94 to 101.   No index

but work is brief enough to be read in one sitting.
This type of reference work unfortunately is often
omitted from most Mexican American bibliographies.   Yet a
catalog to manuscripts is often basic for historical research
and this one was done by an expert.   The 118 items are numbered and described in Spanish; 26 relate specifically to Texas.
There is much dealing with establishment of missions.

52   Castañeda, Carlos Eduardo.   A Report on the Spanish
       Archives in San Antonio, Texas.   Master's thesis,
       University of Texas, Austin, 1923.   349p.
       Summarizes through archives the history of San An-
tonio from its founding to 1830 through land grants, wills and
estates, protocols, lands outside present limits of Bexar
County, and mission records of five missions.   Section labeled miscellaneous has 128 pages.   Arranged as above and
in chronological order.   No subject or name index.
       Most documents date from mid-18th century to 1830's.
Each entry has date, location, brief summary, size and condition of document.   Although documents are in Spanish, entries are in English.

53   Cerda, Gilberto, Berta Cabaza, and Julieta Farias.   Vo-
       cabulario español de Texas.   Austin: University of
       Texas Press, 1953.   347p.
       Presents a regionalistic vocabulary of Spanish in Tex-
as.   Area for selection of vocabulary was eight counties in
south Texas.   The compilers included only words not listed
in the Diccionario de la Academia Española or those they defined in a different way.   Divided into three sections: words
not listed in the Diccionario, idioms not listed in the Diccionario, and hispanismos that the English-speaking of this
region use.
       Lists approximately 2450 words with gender, definition
in Spanish, at times with distinct meanings throughout the
Americas, and often sources for information.   The last two
sections comprise only 100 pages.   Lacking is an introduction describing methodology.   Pronunciation not noted.

54   Chabot, Frederick.   Genealogies of Early San Antonio
       Families: The Makers of San Antonio.   San Antonio,
       Texas: Artes Gráficas, 1937.   412p.
       Genealogical backgrounds of early settlers of San An-
tonio.   Spanish-American, French, Anglo American, and

German.   Presents history of each nationality and then gives
genealogies of major families.   Although he does this for
each of the four groups, the Spanish Americans are by far
the largest.   Organized by nationality.   Table of contents to
Spanish Americans and a type of unalphabetized index that
leads to genealogy of a particular family.
    The work begins with a short 32-page history of the
Spanish Americans in Texas with family background and then
genealogical outlines.   Approximately 100 Spanish-American
families traced.   Chabot used archives of Texas, Mexico,
and Spain as sources.

55   Chabot College Library.   Mexican American Materials.
     Hayward, Cal.:   The Library, 1973.   32p.
     A guide to mainly print materials in this library.
Also some maps.   In spite of title, this bibliography definitely emphasizes Mexico rather than Mexican Americans.   Includes periodicals, newspapers, vertical file materials, and
maps.   The bibliography is then subdivided by topics on
Mexico.   No index or tables of contents.
    448 unannotated articles.   This, like many other bib-
liographies of holdings lists, lacks introductory guidelines.
Mexican American in the title is a misnomer as this is mainly a bibliography on Mexico.   Fails to include some basic
Mexican-American reference works.   Difficult to use because
of lack of index.   In spite of its defects, this bibliography
does include some hints to the user such as subject headings
and vertical file materials.

56   Chapman, Charles E.   Catalogue of materials in the
     Archivo General de Indias for the History of the Pa-
     cific Coast and the American Southwest.   Berkeley:
     University of California Press, 1919.   755p.
     A guide to the archives of Seville for the above-men-
tioned area.   Dates run from 1597 to 1821.   Although title
suggests the entire Southwest, this volume concentrates on
California.   Bundles of documents were selected for their
potential of containing history of California.   Arranged chronologically and each entry has classification number, date,
place, author, function, description of subject matter in English, and finally technical data--i.e., number of copies,
originals, number of pages, amount on a page, cross references, etc.   Topical and name index.
    Innumerable entries on California; at least 144 on New
Mexico, and approximately 170 on Texas.   Arizona also included.

57 Charles, Edgar B. Mexican-American Education: A
      Bibliography. New Mexico State University, 1968,
      ERIC/CRESS. 22p.
      A selective bibliography to be used in meeting the
educational needs of the Mexican American. Includes books,
journal articles and unpublished papers on the following types
of education: preschool, elementary, secondary, higher,
adult, and migrant. All from the 1960's. Arranged alphabetically by author. Subject index.
      90 annotated entries on education of Mexican Ameri-
cans. Each of the large sections indicated above refined to
educational needs; curriculum content; guidance counseling
and vocations; language arts, oral, aural, reading; and inno-
vative programs and practices. Each entry also includes
ERIC number and price of publication. Very good but now
dated.

58 Chávez, Fray Angélico. Archives of the Archdiocese of
      Santa Fe, 1678-1900. Washington, D. C. : Academy
      of American Franciscan History, 1957. 283p.
      Calendar of the material (1678-1900) of the missions
of the Archdiocese of Santa Fe and the material proper to
this diocese. Loose documents, official letters, accounts,
baptisms, marriages, and burials, arranged in this order.
With topical and name index.
      Approximately 3600 documents listed. Information
varies: usually date, one sentence summary, and description
of size. Largest single section on loose documents--i. e. ,
diligencias matrimoniales. Appendix of 20 pages lists friars
and other clergy not found in loose documents.

59 Chávez, Fray Angélico. Origins of New Mexico Families
      in the Spanish Colonial Period in Two Parts: The
      Seventeenth (1598-1821) and the Eighteenth (1693-1821)
      Centuries. Santa Fe: Historical Society of New Mex-
      ico, 1954. 339p.
      Provides a record, although incomplete, of the orig-
inal Spanish families of New Mexico, from 1693 to 1821.
The 17th century included about 130 Spanish soldiers and
their families. The 18th century included the families with
the Vargas Reconquest. In two parts: under each century
the families are alphabetized by surnames.
      Gives genealogies of 155 17th-century families. Each
entry has background of founder of the family, marriages,
births, and references to sources.

60 Chicano/Raza Newspapers and Periodicals, 1965-1972.
    Berkeley, Cal.: Quinto Sol Publications, 1973. De-
    cember 1973. (El Grito Book Series, no. 2.) pp. 57-
    85.
    A serials listing of Chicano newspapers and period-
icals. Bulletins, journals, magazines, newsletters, and
newspapers from 1965-1972, all arranged alphabetically by
title.
    This bibliography is the appendix to Toward a Chicano/
Raza Bibliography: Drama, Prose, Poetry [no. 312]. This useful bibliography lists approximately 150 Chicano newspapers
and periodicals. Each title has address and code indicating
type of publication, address, and then abbreviation of university libraries that have the periodicals and their dates.

61 Cobos, Ruben. Refranes españoles del sudoeste. Span-
    ish Proverbs of the Southwest. Cerrillos, N. M.:
    San Marcos Press, 1973. 144p.
    "... This collection of refranes lends itself to a study
of the psychology, feelings, and attitudes towards life of the
Spanish-speaking people." Refranes from Texas, southern
Colorado, New Mexico, Arizona, and California. Alphabetically arranged by initial word of the refran. Two indexes
integrate the work: first, the key word in Spanish; second,
a listing by topic in English. In other words, this collection
may be used bilingually. However, to locate the key concept
in English may take some searching in the English index.
    1697 refranes in Spanish with English translation.
Cobos begins the collection with an introduction defining the
word refran. The compiler briefly suggests his methodology
in his gratitude to his students who aided him in gathering
these folk sayings. He also lists 25 related works in his
bibliography. An excellent collection that reflects the popular knowledge of the Southwest Mexican Americans. Although
many books on Spanish proverbs exist, this seems to be the
only full-length one on the United States.

62 Colket, Meredith B., and Frank E. Bridgers. Guide to
    Genealogical Records in the National Archives. Wash-
    ington, D. C., 1964. 145p.
    Guide to records of the Federal Government that were
created to satisfy legal requirements or meet administrative
needs but which now have value for genealogical research.
Records in the National Archives from 1790 to ca. 1950.
Census schedules, passenger arrival lists, U.S. military

records, naval and marine records, veterans' benefits, land-
entry records, and other records of genealogical value, arranged in this order. No index but detailed table of contents.
This guide could be one of the best for Mexican American genealogy. Although many of the records do not relate
to this ethnic group, many do--census schedules after 1850,
specific schedules for several of the southwestern states,
and land-entry records for the public-land states. The compilers of the guide warn that the user, the seeker of genealogical materials, must know what type of information the
records contain and how the information is arranged. Generally speaking, these records may be used freely in the National Archives.

63   Colley, Charles C. (comp.). Documents of Southwestern
     History: A Guide to the Manuscript Collection of the
     Arizona Historical Society. Tucson: Arizona His-
     torical Society, 1972. 233p.
     Brings together in complete form a guide to one of
the "largest bodies of historical material available on Arizona,
the American West, and northern Mexico." Over 1000 manuscripts and other original historical documents on the areas
suggested above, arranged alphabetically by surname. Index.
     Although mainly Anglo, this work makes several refer-
ences to Chicanos through the manuscripts of Mexican families. Also indirect references such as guides to cemetery
records, etc. Each entry gives dates, brief description of
items, and also physical size of each, and some biographical
notes.

64   Colorado. General Assembly. Commission on Spanish-
     Surnamed Citizens. The Status of Spanish-Surnamed
     Citizens in Colorado. Denver: The Commission,
     1967. 124p.
     Studies the current problems, needs and conditions of
the Spanish-surnamed population of Colorado: definition, economic status, education, crime and delinquency, health, legal
aid needs, and housing, arranged in that order. No index
but has table of contents.
     Covers this group between the years 1950 and 1960.
Sources were mainly previous studies and interviews with
public officials. Includes 48 tables of statistics, maps, and
charts on multiple aspects of this ethnic group.

65 Coltharp, Mary Lurline. The Tongue of the Tirilones:
   A Linguistic Study of a Criminal Argot. University:
   University of Alabama, 1965. (Alabama Linguistics
   and Philological Series, No. 7.)
   Lists and defines the peculiar Spanish of Caló or the
language of the underworld spoken by the Tirilones. Mainly
lists vocabulary of this jargon from the El Paso border area.
Also provides chapters on anthropological background, informants, phonology and characteristics of Caló.
   The major portion of the book with its chief reference
value is chapter six on vocabulary, which lists approximately
750 words gathered in interviews in 1962 and 1963. Each
entry has definition, number of informants who used it, part
of speech, and symbols indicating its presence in the Diccionario de la lengua española and its inclusion in the works of
other lexicographers. Often the definition is further explained
by use in context.

66 Committee to Recruit Mexican-American Librarians.
   Chicanismo. Los Angeles? 197? 14p.
   Bibliography designed to aid in building a representative Chicano collection. Lists periodicals, books, publishers,
films, and records. Divided into two sections--adult and
children. Final section on periodicals, films, records, and
distributors.
   Very short. Approximately 100 annotated entries on
books. Probably one of the few bibliographies that devotes
a section to children, picture books, fiction, and non-fiction.
Good for a core collection.

67 Conley, Howard K. An Annotated Bibliography of Dissertations on American Indian, Mexican American, Migrant and Rural Education, 1964-72. Las Cruces,
   N.M.: ERIC/CRESS, 1973. 50p. ED 080 251
   Guide to dissertations on the topics suggested in the
title. These are limited to studies in education on the Mexican American and include multiple aspects of this topic:
language, success values, first grade mathematics, etc.
   There are a total of 26 descriptively annotated entries
relating to education and the Mexican American. A subject
index provides easy access. These selections are all from
Dissertation Abstracts.

68 Conmy, Peter Thomas. A Centennial Evaluation of the

Treaty of Guadalupe Hidalgo, 1848-1948. Oakland,
Cal.: Public Library, 1948. 33p.
An explanation of the Treaty of Guadalupe Hidalgo.
Brief background of war, conduct of the war, Trist Mission
to Mexico, and a brief explanation of the 23 articles of the
Treaty of Guadalupe Hidalgo, arranged in this order.   No index or table of contents, because of brevity of work.
An extremely simplified explanation of this treaty written entirely from an Anglo point of view.   Therefore, if possible, this work should be balanced with a Mexican-American
interpretation.   It is a reference work because this treaty
supposedly laid the basis for the U.S. government's relationship to Mexican Americans following the war.

69   Conto, César, and Emiliano Isaza.   Diccionario orto-
      gráfico de apellidos y de nombres propios de personas.
      London: Commercial Bank of Spanish America, 1924.
      149p.
This is a dictionary of baptismal and family names in
Spanish that are often misspelled.   In other words, it tells
nothing of the origin of a name but simply how it should be
spelled according to Spanish tradition.   The compilers have
included 10,280 Spanish names or Hispanicized names.
Of value also is the introductory essay in which the
compilers sketch the main sources for Spanish surnames and
discuss some of the problems concerned in personal names--
spelling changes, the use of de before a name, and custom
of changing a name according to the sex of the bearer.   The
authors also synthesize the evolution of the patronymic system
in Spain.   Conto and Isaza propound an interesting stricture--
i.e., the prohibition of spelling a surname as it pleases the
user for they feel that spelling and etymological rules should
decide the proper writing of a name.   Although this dictionary
could be of value in any Spanish-speaking country, it also is
useful for the Chicano.   For in it are many of the Hispanic
surnames found in the phone directories of cities of Chicano
concentration in the U.S.

70   Conwell, Mary K., and Pura Belpre.   Libros en espanol:
      An Annotated List of Children's Books in Spanish.
      New York: New York Public Library, 1971.   52p.
An annotated list of children's books in Spanish in the
New York Public Library.   Compilers have tried to exclude
all out-of-print materials.   Divided into 11 sections: picture
books; young readers; books for the middle age; books for

older boys and girls; folklore, myths and legends; songs;
games; bilingual books; books for learning Spanish; anthologies; list of sources; and integrated index of authors and
titles.   Approximately 185 annotated titles in the above mentioned categories.
     Since the descriptive annotations are bilingual, this
bibliography is especially unique.   Mexican Americans are
not specified as a theme, but this bibliography would be especially useful to anyone in bilingual programs at the elementary level.   Fiction and non-fiction included and scope is
enormous for it runs from a translation of Alcott's Little
Women to Lazarillo de Tormes to works on astronomy.
Surely one of the best bibliographies for books in Spanish for
children.

71   Cook, Katherine M. , and Florence E. Reynolds.   The
     Education of Native and Minority Groups: A Bibliogra-
     phy, 1932-1934.   Washington, D. C. : U. S. Gov. Print-
     ing Office, 1935.   25p.
     A practical bibliography for students of education.
Covers Indians, Mexican Americans and education in outlying
parts of the United States such as Puerto Rico, Hawaii, etc.
Entries under subject topics.   Table of contents but no index.
     Must be one of the earliest bibliographies on Mexican
Americans and education.   Unfortunately only two and a half
pages dedicated to this topic--or 20 annotated entries.   Mexican Americans included under heading "other minority groups. "
Not really useful as a bibliography but the reduced number of
entries on Mexican Americans perhaps a useful index of the
government's attitude towards this ethnic group at that period.

72   Cook County [Ill.].   Office of Economic Opportunity, Inc.
     Task Force on Spanish-Speaking Affairs.   Planning De-
     partment.   Data on the Spanish American Population
     of Selected Communities of Suburban Cook County,
     Illinois, 1973.   24p.
     Presents information abstracted from the Census Re-
ports for 1970 on the Spanish-American population of Cook
County (i. e. , Chicago).   Includes data on education, occupations, employment of those 16 years and older, income defi-
cit, unemployment, and housing characteristics, arranged in
that order.
     Valuable data on the Spanish speaking in Cook County.
Easy to find similar material for Southwest but generally
more difficult for other areas.   The 1970 Census Reports,

the source for this information, was based on a 15 percent
sampling of the Spanish American population. The only problem is that "Spanish speaking" is never further refined to
Mexican American. Easy-to-read tables often with accompanying explanatory text. 24 municipalities of Cook County included here.

73 Copenhaver, Christina, and Joanne Boelke. Library Ser-
    vice to the Disadvantaged: A Bibliography. Bibli-
    ography Series, No. 1. ERIC Clearing House on Li-
    brary and Information Services, 1968. ED 026 103.
    18p.
    Covers material and library service for the culturally,
economically and educationally deprived in the U.S. and Canada. The 365 entries run from 1960 to 1968 and include
journal and newspaper articles, reports, books, bibliographies,
theses and pamphlets. Divided into four main sections: background and specific aspects; projects and programs; confer-
ences; institutes and workshops; and material lists.
    This is one of the few bibliographies relating to Mexi-
can Americans and library services, an understudied topic
because of its undynamic nature. No one section refers specifically to Mexican Americans; however, several topics under
part I seem relevant: federal legislation and programs, literacy problems, minority groups, and rural disadvantaged.
Many ideas on this topic can be obtained from the section on
projects and programs because here are bibliographies of the
programs of the main public libraries in the U.S. Several
are in regions of Chicano concentration. This bibliography
is now dated but hasn't as yet been superseded.

74 Cordova, Benito. Bibliography of Unpublished Materials
    Pertaining to Hispanic Culture. Santa Fe, N.M.:
    State Department of Education, 1972. ED 086 439
    Guide to material on deposit in the History Library of
the Museum of New Mexico and the State Record Center.
Covers innumerable aspects of Hispanic folkways: corridos,
posadas, witchcraft, curanderismo, furniture, etc. All non-
published materials created under the auspices of the WPA
in the 1930's. All topics integrated into one list organized
by alphabetical entry of author. Excellent subject index and
also index of authors, transcribers and contributors.
    This is a guide to fresh material recently rediscovered
because of the interest in folklore and oral history. It is invaluable for any one interested in the folkways of the Hispanic

peoples of New Mexico.   Each entry has: number, author,
title, subject and one-sentence summary, and number of
words.   Material is available at the two places indicated at
the top.

75   Cordova, Gilberto.   Terms Indigenous to New Mexico
        Hispanos [xerox copy].   n. p. , n. d.
        A guide to Spanish words that have a peculiarly re-
gional meaning in New Mexico.   No accompanying text so no
regional limitations established.   One must assume that New
Mexico refers to the entire state.   Words seem to be derived
either from Mexico or Spain.   No indication that some could
be New Mexican Indian.   Alphabetical arrangement.
        Approximately 225 words listed.   Each entry gives
only the meaning with occasional cross references.   No syl-
labification or suggestion as to word origin or use in a sentence.   Mainly nouns.   Unfortunately no introduction or guide
to methodology and sources.   Since this work is still in manuscript form, perhaps the author never completed a very
necessary introduction.   In spite of defects, this is a contribution to a neglected area.

76   Cortez, Rubén.   Mexican-American History: A Critical
        Selective Bibliography.   Santa Barbara, Cal. : Mexi-
        can American Historical Society, 1969.   20p.
        The purpose is to help teachers give meaning to their
subject and make available the most useful books.   Depicts
la raza chronologically, Indian, Spanish, and Mexican and
finally goes into experience in the United States.   Arranged
by race and by historical experience.   No index.
        Approximately 240 sporadically annotated entries.   The
extremely broad chronological and cultural scope is perhaps
too ambitious for 20 pages.

77   Cotera, Martha P. (comp.).   Educator: Guide to Chi-
        cano Resources.   Crystal City, Texas: Crystal City
        Memorial Library, 1971.   58p?
        Guide to multi-media resources for educators and li-
brarians.   Strictly Mexican American and almost totally 20th
century.   Arranged alphabetically within sections by format.
Table of contents but no index.
        Over 400 entries on books, reports, pamphlets, jour-
nals, newspapers, films, filmstrips, tapes, records, and
posters.   The entries are normally unannotated.   The main

value of this guide is listing the price and the distributor of
the materials for easy ordering.   Would be very valuable for
high school, junior high teachers and public librarians.   The
monographs listed might be considered a core collection.

78   Coy, Owen C.   Guide to the County Archives of Cali-
       fornia.   Sacramento: California State Printing Office,
       1919.   622p.
       Guide to county archives and handbook.   Consideration
and care of records, general description of records, complete
list of all sets of records in the custody of the more important officers of the county, history of changes in the territorial jurisdiction of the various counties.   Two parts: care
and use, and guide to county archives.   The counties presented alphabetically.   Subject index.
       59 counties listed.   Each with introduction, court
records, supervisors' records, naturalization, elections, marriage and public health, private business concerns, superintendent of schools, etc.   Some of the counties also have pre-
statehood records.   The information mainly tells of the existence of the records and gives dates and volume number.
Enough clues are present to lead one to Spanish records.
Naturally other categories such as naturalization and marriage would lead to Mexican-American records.

79   Cumberland, Charles C.   The United States-Mexican
       Border: A Selective Guide to the Literature of the
       Region.   New York: Arno Press, 1974.   236p.
       A guide for researchers to the unique region that di-
vides and unites two cultures.   Almost all aspects of the
Mexican-American border since Mexican independence.   Books,
articles, government publications, theses and unpublished
manuscripts.   Covers diplomatic relations, descriptions,
Spanish-speaking population of the U. S., immigration from
Mexico, history, education, land use, economic activity, aspects of culture, government and politics, and the Indians of
the border area, arranged in this order.   Each section subdivided by format.   Table of contents and index to authors.
       This is a 1974 reprint of a 1960 bibliography.   Prob-
ably the best bibliography on the borderlands to date.   Cumberland's work is an example of the attainments possible within the art of bibliography.   He has not only examined but
understood each item under consideration within its historical
context.   Each section is prefaced by a synthesizing essay on
the bibliographic maturity of the field.   This is followed by

entries with cogent prescriptive summaries of 115 journals
consulted.   Invaluable for understanding the Mexican American of the border area.   A subject index would have facilitated use for entry and for cross indexing.

80   Curry, Mary Margaret.   The World of Mexican Cooking:
     A Collection of Delicious and Authentic Recipes from
     South of the Border.   Los Angeles: Nash Pub. Co. ,
     1971.   101p.
     Recipes of Mexican food as it is prepared in South
Texas.   Covers Mex-Tex food only and does not refer to
Mexican food as it is prepared in other Southwestern states.
Divided into 11 chapters: world of Mexican cooking, basic
recipes, party foods, tortillas, enchiladas, main course
dishes, Mex-Tex food, American recipes influenced by Tex-
Mex cooking, desserts and menus.   Table of contents.
     Extremely practical cookbook that presents Mexican
recipes influenced by Texas.   Although only one chapter deals
specifically with Tex-Mex recipes, almost the whole work relates to Texas.   Author gives helpful hints and easy directions.   Probably one of the few Mexican cookbooks dealing
mainly with Texas.

81   Curtin, LSM.   Healing Herbs of the Upper Rio Grande.
     Santa Fe, N. M. :   Laboratory of Anthropology, 1947.
     281p.
     To catalogue and describe the medicinal herbs of this
area of Hispanic settlement.   Includes both history and use
of approximately 300 herbs, arranged alphabetically.   Two
indexes provide easy access to this work: an herb index and
a remedy index (i. e. , looking up the ailment, one is referred
to the appropriate herb remedy).
     This is more than just a catalog, for Curtin identifies
the herb in Spanish, then gives an English and Latin translation.   The description, often a page in length, includes the
history plus interesting folkloric elements of the Spanish of
New Mexico.

82   DeAnza College.   Library.   Chicanos--Relevance Now:
     Mexican American Bibliography.   Cupertino, Cal. :
     DeAnza College Library, 1970.   6p.
     Apparently a minimal holding list on Mexican-Ameri-
can studies in DeAnza College.   Only monographs in social
science and literature.   Mainly Mexican Americans with an

emphasis on California. Some titles on Mexico. Arrangement is alphabetical by author.
  101 unannotated entries. As with many bibliographies,
this one suffers from lack of an introduction giving guidelines
for use. One therefore wonders at the occasional appearance
of a title from Mexico and the exclusion of perhaps significant works. The only value is as a guide to the holdings of
DeAnza College Library as no new titles are mentioned.

83 Delgado, Lucy. Comidas de New Mexico. Santa Fe,
      N. M. : n. p. , 1967. 31p.
      Presents recipes of the traditional dishes of New Mex-
ico. Has a cross section of all types of dishes and also has
Anglo dishes. Alphabetical index.
      Has the defect of most New Mexican recipe books in
that it does not define Hispanic food. Approximately 70 recipes. Only difference from other New Mexico cookbooks is
the suggestion of Anglo influence in some of the recipes,
e. g. , German beer, orange cottage cheese salad, etc.

84 Denver Public Library. Mexican Heritage: A Selected
      Book List for All Ages. Denver: n. p. , 1970? 34p.
      Presents only a portion of Mexican materials of the
Denver Public Library for all age levels. Has materials on
Mexican Americans but also many works on Mexico. Mainly
in English but also a short list of works in Spanish. Books
and audiovisual materials. Divided into two sections, adult
and young adult and children.
      Lists approximately 200 items. Each with author,
title, call number and short descriptive annotation. A popular guide with no pretenses of exhaustiveness or specialization.

85 Diaz, Albert James. A Guide to the Microfilm of Papers
      Relating to New Mexico Land Grants. Albuquerque:
      University of New Mexico Press, 1960. 102p.
      Describes and classifies the different types of records
of New Mexico land grants. Four major categories--docu-
ments described in Twitchell (q. v.), various indexes and
record books maintained prior to the establishment of the
office of Surveyor General, records of the Surveyor General
of New Mexico and records of the Court of Private Land
Claims, arranged in this order. Earliest date seems to be
1721. Has table of contents, summary of arrangement of

papers, and index to claims adjudicated by U.S. Surveyor
General and U.S. Court of Private Land Claims.
     As author states, this guide is mainly a finding device
and gives little information about individual cases. In addition to table of contents, also a guide to arrangement of papers that presents 23 subdivisions of records and appropriate
pages in this guide. Most of the names, both personal and
community, are of Spanish origin. This is an invaluable initial tool for studying land claims.

86 Diaz, Carmen. Bilingual-Bicultural Materials. Lawrence,
     Kan. : Special Education Instructional Materials Center,
     1973. 93p. ED 084 915
     "Describes educational materials which are both bi-
lingual and bicultural. It also lists evaluative instruments
which can be useful in making assessments of children who
come from Spanish speaking families." Divided into sections:
English as a foreign language, mathematics, music, reading,
science, social studies, Spanish as a foreign language, evaluation instruments, descriptions of curriculum projects, and
bibliographies. Has 88 well-annotated entries with: title,
developer, publisher, format, description, and comments.
     The section on comments is of particular interest be-
cause it suggests the limitations of the work and the special
needs of the teacher. Description is refined to: grade level,
curricular area, peripheral usefulness, culture, and purpose.
Most of the entries seem to be for the elementary level.
Highly recommended because of its detailed yet easily accessible evaluations.

87 Directory. Hispanic Congregations. Pastors. Ameri-
     can Baptist Churches [mimeographed]. Valley Forge,
     Pa. : 1974? 8p.
     Directory of pastors with Spanish surnames in the
American Baptist Church in Ariz. , Cal. , Colo. , Conn. , Fla. ,
Ill. , Ind. , Kan. , Mass. , Mich. , Mo. , Neb. , N.J. , N.Y. ,
Pa. , Wis. , and Mexico.
     Arranged alphabetically, this is a guide to approxi-
mately 160 Hispanic congregations and pastors in the United
States and Mexico. Each entry gives pastor's name, ad-
dress, and church. Indicated also is whether congregation
is Spanish speaking.

88 Documents of the Chicano Struggle. New York: Path-

finder Press, 1971. 15p.
Intended to make available to everyone the (Spiritual)
Plan of Aztlan, its organizational goals and action. This
brief publication also includes the program of the Raza Unida
Party of the Oakland area.
This is a basic document of one of the militant wings
of Chicanismo. The first document, El Plan de Aztlan, is
a general statement of goals; the second, the Raza Unida
Party Program, details objectives--political, economic, educational, and Raza women's platform. Very short document
that summarizes the needs of the Chicanos.

89   Drake, Eugene B.   Compilation of Spanish Grants.   San
     Francisco: Kenny and Alexander, 1861. 68p.
Presents a list of land grants mainly to Spanish surnamed persons in California from 1830 to 1846. The title
of this work refers to Drake's incorporation of several earlier titles on land grants into one compilation: Jimeno's and
Hartnell's Indexes of Land Concessions, from 1830 to 1846;
Approvals of Land Grants by the Territorial Deputation and
Departmental Assembly of California, from 1835 to 1846,
and A List of Unclaimed Grants. Drake subdivides this work
into approvals, certificates of surveyor general, explanatory
notes, grants unclaimed, Hartnell's Index, Jimeno's Index,
Toma de razon, and unclaimed grants.
This is a compilation of various sources relating to
land grants of California. Since it precedes the Gold Rush
years and the Anglo influx, it contains many Spanish surnames. Many of the entries are chronological and have entry number, date, location of grant, and name of the holder
of the grant. This work could be considered early Mexican
American or when California belonged to Mexico. It is useful for California history from a Chicano perspective and for
genealogy of the Spanish surnamed.

90   Duran, Daniel Flores.   Venceremos con libros y la
     lengua.   Richmond, Cal. : Richmond Public Library,
     1969. 9p.   ED 070 501
Bibliography of this library's collection of materials
in Spanish, and materials in English on the problems and culture of the Spanish speaking. Covers magazines, dictionaries,
and books, and phonograph records. Arranged by format,
then topic.
A very short bibliography but commendable for its
emphasis on Spanish-language materials. The compiler ac-

cepts the reality that many Mexican Americans are not interested in Chicano literature but may want works from Spanish
America or what is more likely, translations of English fav-
orites or the classics.   Like the bibliography for the Oakland
library, (see under Oakland Public Library), this one fills an
area neglected in most other bibliographies.   The citations on
books in English do not contribute as much.

91   Duran, Patricia Herrera.   The Chicana: A Preliminary
        Bibliographical Study.   Los Angeles: University of
        California.   Chicano Studies Center, 1973? unpaged.
        Attempts to collect available material on the Chicana;
not limited to the Chicana but covers women in general.   Includes diverse topics such as criminality, women's liberation,
child-rearing, etc.   Mainly 20th century.   Seven sections--
books, documents and papers, articles, theses and dissertations, films, newspapers, and index.
        The 273 entries are generally without annotations.
Scope is too broad and list should be refined to works that
are specifically on Chicanas.   Does not include la Chicana in
creative literature.   In spite of defects, this bibliography
could serve as a useful beginning.

92   Eastern New Mexico University.   Library.   A Selected
        List of Materials Relating to Mexican-Americans.
        Portales, N. M. :   Eastern New Mexico University,
        1970.
        A cross section of all print materials relating to Mexi-
can Americans in the library of Eastern New Mexico University.   Monographs and government documents on Mexico and
Mexican Americans, mainly from the point of view of social
science.   Integrated list arranged alphabetically.   No index.
        Over 300 unannotated entries.   Guidelines are not well
drawn so this list in many ways is more Mexican than Mexican American.   Unfortunately it includes no bibliographies or
indexes or abstracts so it leaves the user with few additional
sources.   Its list of subject headings is mainly of Mexican
topics.   No journal articles or theses or non-print materials.

93   Edington, Everett D. , and Lewis Tamblyn (comps.).   Re-
        search Abstracts in Rural Education.   Las Cruces,
        N. M. :   Clearinghouse on Rural Education and Small
        Schools, 1969.   70p.
        Designed "to acquaint the rural educator with some of

the latest research and development findings in his field. "
ERIC reports on rural education, small schools, Indian education, Mexican American education, migrant education, and
outdoor education, arranged in this order.   Topical index.
          Approximately 120 entries.   Each with microfiche code
number, title, author, publication date and 140-word descriptive abstract.   20 of these relate specifically to Mexican
Americans; others mainly relate or are peripheral.   Very useful for educators without access to computer searches of
ERIC files.

94   Educational Testing Service.   Graduate and Professional
       School Opportunities for Minority Students.   4th ed.
       Princeton, N. J. , 1972.   113p.
          Helps minority students in their awareness and search
for graduate and professional school opportunities.   Provides
summaries of these opportunities in the United States.   Data
probably gathered in 1971 for fields of business, law, medicine, and general graduate education.   Includes source of
funds for minority students, qualifying examinations for entrance, graduate schools, graduate departments, law schools,
business schools, and medical schools, arranged in this order.   Index and table of contents.
          320 graduate schools and 576 graduate departments and
professional schools listed.   Each with: person to contact,
application fee, tests used, application dates, number of students, minority students and minority faculty members.   Graduate departments run alphabetically from American studies to
zoology.   Highly pertinent information for any Mexican American considering graduate school opportunities.

95   Elac, John Chala.   The Employment of Mexican Workers
       in U. S. Agriculture, 1900-1960:   A Binational Eco-
       nomic Analysis.   Los Angeles: University of Califor-
       nia, 1961.   152p.
          Intended to present an economic analysis of labor mo-
bility on a binational basis.   As title suggests, author incorporates labor from 1900 to 1960.   Covers diverse topics such
as entry of Mexican labor into U. S. , history of labor legislation, agricultural economy of the U. S. , development in Mexican economy since 1900 and the economics of the bracero
program, arranged in this order.   Also contains 29 statistical tables, a nine-page bibliography but no index.
          Very concise view of a complex topic.   Elac's theory
is that the international boundary between employer and em-

ployee interposes a political factor. Consequently, economic
analysis is complicated by political factors. 29 separate
graphs illuminate the text. Elac's long bibliography suggests
a thorough coverage of the topic. Synthesizes much scat-
tered information.

96 Eldredge, Zoeth S. The Spanish Archives of California.
      (Paper read before the California Genealogical Society,
      July 13, 1901.) San Francisco: Murdock Press, 1901.
      8p.
      Brief description of California archives only, none
later than about 1833, in the custody of the United States Surveyor General. Also several paragraphs on the colonization
of California to aid in understanding the archives.
      Tells what these archives may contain, e.g., monthly
reports from the presidio, reports from padres. Definitely
not a calendar but an early description of the potential of the
Spanish archives.

97 Elliot, Claude. Theses on Texas History: A Check List
      of Theses and Dissertations in Texas History Produced
      in the Department of History of Eighteen Texas Gradu-
      ate Schools and Thirty-Three Graduate Schools Outside
      of Texas, 1907-1952. Austin: Texas State Historical
      Assoc., 1955. 280p.
      Reveals what studies have been done in Texas history
and serves as a research source for scholars. Inclusions ex-
tend beyond history as list of abbreviations of classification
refers to 84 subdivisions that impinge on other disciplines.
Name and topic index.
      Lists 652 such studies. Each entry has author, de-
gree, year, length of work, degree-granting institution, collation, descriptive paragraph, and topics covered in work.
Over 70 entries on Mexicans in Texas.

98 El Paso (Texas) Public Schools. Bilingual Bicultural
      Materials; A Listing for Library Resource Centers.
      El Paso, Texas: El Paso Public Schools, 1974. 79p.
      Developed from "a desire to identify and evaluate ma-
terials of potential value to learning resource centers serving bilingual bicultural programs...." Covers all formats--
sound filmstrips, recordings, kits, slides, games and books,
arranged in this order. Refers mainly to Spanish speaking.
Table of contents but no index.

Approximately 350 entries.   Each with bibliographical
information and excellent prescriptive annotations.   Also
gives appropriate grade level for each item, most are for
elementary and junior high.   Broad variety of formats.   Ex-
cellence of this bibliography is probably due to the contributions of 80 school teachers.   This bibliography would be indispensable for any elementary or junior high librarian who
works with Mexican-American children.

99   Institute of Labor and Industrial Relations (University of
     Michigan--Wayne State University).   Research Division.
     Document and Reference Text; An Index to Minority
     Group Employment Information.   Detroit, 1967.
     602p.
     "An index to literature relating to employment and em-
ployment-related problems of major categories of minority
workers covered under Title VII of the Civil Rights Act of
1964. "   Monographs and periodicals from 1956 to 1966.
Negro Americans, Spanish-speaking Americans (Puerto Rican
and Mexican American), American Indians, Oriental Americans, and women.   Also agencies administering fair employment practice acts and organizations concerned with minority
group employment.   Entries under key words.   At the end
of the book is the list of these key words.   User could find
the same title on Mexican Americans entered under several
different key words.   Introduction gives careful explanation
of use.
     Probably the most complete bibliography that exists
on minority group employment.   Produced under contract
with the Equal Employment Opportunity Commission.   Chicanos could be found under Mexican American, Spanish speaking,
minority, the various southwestern states, migrants, women,
etc.   In other words, the user has to try several headers to
make a complete search.   For example, if Mexican American not in the title, the entry could appear under some other
label.   All entries unannotated.   Many labels suggest topics
peripheral to the Mexican Americans.   A 1971 supplement was
issued in one volume, Joe A. Miller and Steven C. Gold, eds.

100   Ericson, Carolyn Reeves.   Nacogdoches--Gateway to
      Texas; A Biographical Directory, 1773-1849.   Fort
      Worth, Texas: 1974.   248p.
      To make available the records of Nacogdoches for the
genealogist.   Heretofore this data has been comparatively inaccessible.   Covers entrance certificates of 1835; census

records 1792-1809, 1828-1835 and 1847; tax lists of 1839,
1840, and 1845; early marriage records; cemetery records;
Nacogdoches County deeds from 1836 to 1849, etc. The body
of the book is the biographical directory of inhabitants: two
appendices of early documents and immigration laws and decrees. Table of contents and index of family dependents who
are included under heads of households. A three-page bibliography.

　　Apparently this directory unites genealogical data from
diverse sources. Approximately 4280 surnames are mentioned. Data varies from each entry--marriage, origin of
data, occupation, deaths, religion, parentage, burial place,
nationality and organizational affiliation. Perhaps one-third
of the names suggest Spanish origin. Invaluable guide to
genealogists.

101　Everton, Sr. George B. and Gunnar Rasmuson. Handy
　　　Book for Genealogists. Logan, Utah: Everton Pub-
　　　lishers, 1965. 220p.

　　This book is a primer for the amateur genealogists
for it states the value of state histories, county histories,
location of genealogical libraries, maps of value, county
records, and a check list of the Historical Records Survey.
The compilers arranged the book alphabetically by state, and
under each state will be found valuable information for the
genealogists: brief history of the state; location of vital statistics, naturalization records, deeds for real estate, genealogical collections; and an alphabetical listing of state counties with dates formed, population size, census reports available, parent county, and county seat. Ariz., Cal., Colo.,
N.M., and Texas also included and with the above genealogical information.

　　Any searcher for records of Mexican Americans in
the United States would want to rely on this primer. Very
useful is the listing of counties and dates in order to find
county records. In other words this work leads the researcher to many secondary and primary sources of genealogical
information.

102　Farias, María Julieta. The Spanish Language in Texas.
　　　No. 3 Duval, Webb, and Zapata Counties. Master's
　　　thesis, University of Texas, Austin. 1950. 122p.

　　To note the peculiarities of the Spanish vocabulary in
these three Texas counties. Includes vocabulary, idiomatic
sayings and proverbs and hispanismos incorporated into the

speech of the Anglos.
      Lists approximately 350 Spanish words. Each has
gender, meaning in these three counties of Texas, and meaning in other parts of the Hispanic world.   Part II made up
of 200 sayings common to the area.   The final section con-
sists of a short list of Spanish words used by Anglos.   A
defect of the work is the lack of an introduction outlining
scope and procedures.

103   Fellows, Lloyd.   Economic Aspects of the Mexican
       Rural Population in California with Special Emphasis
       on the Need for Mexican Labor in Agriculture (1929).
       San Francisco: R and E Research Assoc., 1971.
       95p.
      A study designed for those interested in the agricul-
tural development of California.   It attempts to survey the
entire field of Mexican labor in California and to show the
relationship between immigration and the need for farm labor.
Mainly early 20th century.   Besides five chapters of text
describing the problem, this study also contains 38 tables of
statistics.   Arrangement: racial and historical background
on the Mexican agricultural worker, Mexican labor in Mexico,
the growth of California's agriculture, the need for Mexican
labor in California agriculture, and Mexican immigration.
Detailed table of contents but no index.
      The main value of this study is as an early effort at
analysis of the Mexican and agriculture in California.   As
such it contains several embarrassing racial biases.   Lacking
is a detailed discussion of methodology.   Perhaps both defects reflect the status of the field of statistics in the 1920's.
However, the bibliography does indicate 12 primary sources
where statistics were gathered.   Good for tables on costs of
living in various states of Mexico and tables on Mexicans in
California.   Though primitive these are probably the only
statistics from the 1920's.

104   Fergusson, Erna.   Mexican Cookbook.   Albuquerque:
       University of New Mexico Press, 1973.   118p.
      Presents recipes "which were in common use when the
province of New Mexico was a part of the Republic of Mexico.
They represent Mexican cookery that belongs to the United
States."   In addition to having the standard entries for recipe
books--e.g., spices, soups, breads--this work also attempts
to provide the regional background for New Mexican cookery.
Has a table of contents and index.

Of the Mexican American cookbooks evaluated in this bibliography, Mexican Cookbook is one of the oldest, coming out first in 1934. This is one of the few wherein the author states that adaptation to native Mexican food took place in New Mexico. Over 100 recipes with clear instructions. Along with Philomena Romero's work (q. v.) this is one of the best on New Mexican food.

105 Flaxman, Erwin. A Selected Bibliography on Teacher
     Attitudes. New York: Columbia University, ERIC
     Clearinghouse on the Urban Disadvantaged, 1969. 23p.
     ED 027 357
     "Some of the works ... present the findings of studies identifying the racial and social attitudes of the middle class urban teacher and indicate how these attitudes may affect student performances. " Has 29 descriptively annotated entries that relate to teacher attitude, teacher characteristics and background, behavior and education. Each of the 29 entries has abstract length evaluations.
     This bibliography supplements the many bibliographies in education for it is one of the few that concerns a neglected aspect in the improvement of the education of the Mexican American, i.e. , teacher attitude. At least five of the entries relate to the Southwest and the others certainly are relevant to the teachers of the Mexican American. Although short, this bibliography has a table of contents and a subject index combined.

106 Flesher, Lorna. American Minorities; A Checklist of
     Bibliographies Published by Government Agencies,
     1960-1970. Sacramento: California State Library,
     Government Publications Section, 1970. 7p.
     Lists bibliographies on American Indians, Oriental Americans, Mexican Americans, and Black Americans in that order. Too brief to need table of contents or index.
     Has eight annotated bibliographies on Mexican Americans and perhaps three additional ones listed under General. Lists some works that are standard entries in most bibliographies and several that are relatively unknown. The major defect is lack of introductory explanation as to methodology or criteria for selection. Apparently government publications here refer to those issued by the U. S. government and the California state government.

107   Fodell, Beverly.   César Chávez and the United Farm
       Workers; A Selective Bibliography.   Detroit: Wayne
       State University Press, 1974.   103p.
       "Provides those interested in César Chávez and the
United Farm Workers and the various aspects of the grape
and lettuce strikes and attendant boycotts, with a wide selection of readily available published materials.... " Main emphasis is on recent (since 1965) attempts to organize.   Covers all print materials--monographs, articles, government
documents, reports and position papers, dissertations and
theses; arranged by format; no index.
       Approximately 1400 entries, many annotated.   The
source of this bibliography, Wayne State University, was de-
signated in 1967 as the official depository of the United Farm
Workers Organizing Committee.   Although many other bibliographies refer to labor, this is the only one dedicated to the
Mexican-American farm laborer.   The introduction summarizes each category of materials and recommends certain
items.   Many entries may be peripheral.   Especially valuable
to the general user are the five pages on Chicano bibliography.   The main defect of this work is the absence of an index.

108   Frey, Ed, Jr. (comp.).   Migrant Services Directory.
       Michigan: n.p. , 1969.   44p.
       Directory of services available to migrant workers in
Michigan.   Mainly for the year 1969, so perhaps dated now.
Includes: civil rights commissions, health care, legal services, social security, vocational rehabilitation, etc.   Table
of contents lists 17 different agencies or activities of potential use for the migrant in Michigan.
       This is a bilingual English/Spanish edition.   Highly
useful to anyone in the migrant labor force.   Probably this
reference work is of more value, however, to organizations
or persons interested in improving the conditions of migrant
laborers.

109   Frishman, Nettie (comp.).   Between Two Cultures:
       Children's Books about Mexican-American and Chil-
       dren in Mexico [xerox copy?].   Los Angeles: L. A.
       Public Library, 1969.   13p.
       Apparently a cross section of young people's books
(only) on Mexicans and Mexican Americans at the LAPL, to
1969.   "Children" here defined as pre-school through junior
high school.   All books in English.   Alphabetized by author

under different age categories of potential users.
There are 76 annotated titles.   Each entry has a descriptive annotation and a note as to whether it is Mexican
or Mexican American.   Approximately one half of these are
on Mexican Americans.   Two supplements somewhat update
this list--Chicanitos by Jose G. Taylor in 1974, and Libros
para los niños by Laura Aldredge and Walfrido Lamotte.   One
perhaps can hope soon for a large integrated bibliography with
bilingual entries for the holdings of the public library in one
of the cities in the U.S. with a large-Spanish speaking population.

110   Galvan, Robert Arispe.   El dialecto español de San An-
        tonio, Tejas.   Ph. D. dissertation, Tulane University,
        New Orleans, 1954.   314p.
        Attempts to localize and note the uniqueness of the
Spanish language of San Antonio, Texas.   Contains 940 words
in dictionary arrangement and an analysis of each one; limited
to city of San Antonio.
        Excellent introduction sets the limits of the work.
Each of the 900 entries has: spelling, accent, part of speech,
etymology, meaning of the word in San Antonio, example of
meaning in context, and geographical distribution outside of
San Antonio.   Also has 14-page bibliography.

111   Galvan, Robert A. and Richard V. Teschner.   El dic-
        cionario español de Tejas.   The Dictionary of the
        Spanish of Texas.   Silver Spring, Md. :   Institute of
        Modern Languages, 1975.   102p.
        The authors attempt to include all of the Spanish
words in Texas that are not found in the more standard dictionaries.   They themselves refer to their compilation as a
supplement to these better known works.   Confining themselves to Texas, Galvan and Teschner, applying this criterion, have found almost 7000 entries, taken from secondary
sources relating to the Spanish language in Texas and then
processed by computer.   Those found in already established
works were excluded.   Information on entries varies.   All
have the minimum--spelling and definition--but the authors
list 62 abbreviations that suggest that sporadically more information is offered.   Unavailable are pronunciation and sub-
regional location within Texas.
        This work, compared to what is available in regional
dictionaries, is superior: it is one of the few in which the
authors discuss methodology and goals; they list over fifty

sources in their bibliography; they include street language;
and finally their work is in a convenient format that should
make it available to all libraries and laymen. They also include seven pages of proverbs heard in Texas but not limited
to this state and a one-page explanation of verb conjugations.
This is a valuable reference work for both the specialist and
the non-specialist.

112 Gamio, Manuel. Quantitative Estimate: Sources and
     Distribution of Mexican Immigration into the United
     States. México: Tallares Gráficos Editorial y "Di-
     ario Oficial," 1930. 49p.
     Presents statistics on migration of Mexicans into the
U. S. , 1920-1928, and their regional origin in Mexico; location
in the U. S. of Mexican immigrants for the same year; a-
mount of money sent for these years; and states in Mexico
where money was sent. Some text but mainly statistics and
graphs in the above order.
     This is an early study on Mexican immigration be-
tween the two countries. Apparently it was prompted by fear
of the U. S. that too many Mexicans were entering the U. S.
and the fear of Mexico that it was losing too many economically productive workers. The author has based his figures
mainly on Mexican sources--the record of money orders sent
from the U. S. to Mexico. Each has sender city of U. S. , receiving city in Mexico, date, amount of money, name of
sender and recipient. From this unique source the author
has compiled his statistics and his theory on returnees. Invaluable information on origin of immigrants and their location in the U. S.

113 Genealogical Periodical Annual. Index. 1962- .
     This annual publication indexes genealogical informa-
tion from 124 periodicals from the U. S. , Canada, and the
British Isles. Entries may be found under surname or under
state and include subject, years and abbreviation of periodical
with date and pages. All of the Southwestern states are listed and under them, entries of Chicano interest. For example, in the 1967 issue under Texas is entered: "Bexar
Co[unty] San Antonio cem[etery] burial rec[ord]s. 1879 OH
9:1:2. " Other topics suggested by the abbreviations are: an-
cestors, marriage, pensions, descendants, etc. This is
probably the only bibliographical control over genealogical
sometimes hidden in periodicals. Though mainly Anglo, much
here is of value for the Chicanos--information unavailable

from other sources. The last volume was published in 1973
and covers the year 1969.

114 Gilbert, Fabiola C. Historic Cookery. Las Vegas,
     N. M.: La Galeria de los Artesanos, 1970. 43p.
     Presents "real New Mexican dishes." Limited to New
Mexico but includes a cross section of Hispanic foods. Arranged by type of food--i. e., sauces, corn dishes, meats,
soups, etc. Table of contents indicating type of food as suggested above. Also index in Spanish with English translation.
     One of few cookbooks that indirectly attempts to de-
scribe Hispanic food of New Mexico, for the author lists the
basic foods of New Mexico. Has 117 recipes, so is one of
larger compilations. In addition to the normal format of ingredients and instructions, Gilbert also gives occasional introductory notes to recipes that present some of the cultural
history of the foods. One of better cookbooks for New Mexico.

115 Godoy Alcantara, D. José. Ensayo histórico etimológico
     filológico sobre los apellidos castellanos. Madrid: M.
     Rivadeneyra, 1871. 280p.
     The author presents a discussion as well as a per-
sonal name dictionary of Spanish names. He includes: history of the Castillian surname; names formed from geographical places; names inspired by religious beliefs; names orig-
inally formed to indicate social status or civilian or military
employment; names formed from the state or condition of the
individual, i. e., age, relationship, profession, defects, personal qualities and nicknames; use of the de before the surname; and foreign names. The study is arranged in this order and unfortunately has no index to lead one directly to a
particular surname.
     By far the largest section of this work is devoted to
names derived from place names. He often writes a paragraph on each name tracing it back to a Latin root. Godoy
Alcantara does not list as many names as Tibón's Diccionario
(q. v.) or the Alvarez work (q. v.), but he introduces his dictionary with a 60-page discussion on the history of names and
for this reason is an excellent supplement to the others. As
in the other name dictionaries, many Mexican-American
names are included.

116 Gómez-Quiñónes, Juan. Selected Materials for Chicano

Studies. Austin: University of Texas, 29p.
Apparently the list includes all disciplines at the University of Texas. Organized by generalities and also disciplines, i. e. , Mexican heritage. No index or table of contents. Topics alphabetically arranged.
The approximately 400 unannotated entries include both
monographs and articles. The compiler provides no guidelines as to scope or arrangement of materials. Appears to
be a cross section on Mexico, the Mexican American, and
Southwest history of U. S. In addition to the general section,
materials are also entered under U. S. context, economics
and labor, education, folklore and mythology, history, law
and justice, literature, migration, political science, psychology, public health and Mexican literature. Commendable is
the last section because it concerns the Chicano viewed in
Mexican novels and theatre. In general this bibliography is
inferior to Gómez-Quiñones and Camarillo's Selected Bibliography (q. v.).

117 Gómez-Quiñónes, Juan. Selective Bibliography on Chi-
     cano Labor Materials. n. p. , n. d. 3p.
A selection of mainly monographs, government documents, and some articles relating to Mexican Americans and
labor, 1908 to 1972. No newspapers or dissertations. No
apparent organization.
Has 47 unannotated entries. Three types of materials
were selected for this bibliography--labor in Mexico, Mexican-American laborers, and labor problems in general. The
compiler provides no introduction. Surely many more articles
must exist on Chicano labor. No bibliographies listed or
guides to fair employment practices. This work may be sup-
plemented by:

118 Gómez-Quiñónes, Juan, and Alberto Camarillo. Select-
     ed Bibliography for Chicano Studies. Los Angeles:
     University of Southern California, Chicano Studies Cen-
     ter, 1974.
Inclusive bibliography that updates previous works.
Includes both periodicals and monographs. No annotations or
index. Broad in time and culture--i. e. , begins with history
in 1598 and finishes with 1973: bibliographies, statistical
materials, journals, general, Mexican heritage, U. S. context,
economics and labor, education, folklore, history, law and
justice, literature, migration, political science, psychology,
public health, sociology/anthropology, women, and Mexican

writings.   Arranged alphabetically by subject.   No index.
Probably the most recent bibliography.   Has 19 sections with approximately 600 unannotated entries.   This is a
superior bibliography not just for its scope but its excellent
cross-section of materials; e.g., it includes topics often subsumed by other disciplines: statistics, psychology and women.   These bibliographies do not emphasize Mexico (27 entries relate to this country).   The chapter on history is well
handled in that most of the items relate both to Mexico and
the United States.   For a library that cannot afford multiple
bibliographies on Mexican Americans, this one would be a
wise choice.

119   Gonzáles, Jesús J. (comp.).   Bibliography of Mexican
      American Studies on Various Subjects [mimeographed].
      San Bernardino, Cal.:   San Bernardino Valley College,
      1971.   21p.
      Apparently a guide to the works on Mexico and the
Mexican American that are in the San Bernardino Valley College
Library.   Mainly monographs but also Mexican-American
newspapers.   Art, economy, history, literature, philosophy,
political science, psychology, religion, and sociology.   Entries are alphabetized within these separate disciplines.   No
index or table of contents.
      All entries unannotated.   Aside from the newspapers
listed, this bibliography could with little inaccuracy be labeled a bibliography of Mexican studies.   Very few entries
relate to the Mexican American.   The author gives no guidelines as to the scope of his study.   Notably lacking are entries on Mexican-American bibliographies.

120   Goodman, Mary Ellen, and Don des Jarlais.   The Span-
      ish Surname Population of Houston; A Demographic
      Sketch.   Houston, Texas: Rice University, Center for
      Research in Social Change and Economic Development,
      1968.   21p.
      "An attempt to give a demographic portrait valid for
1965," for the Spanish surname population of Houston.   Contains: Basic statistics on Mexican Americans in Houston for
1965--population growth, average annual net migration, de-
pendency ratios, age group percentages, income, employment,
education, housing, and segregation, arranged in this order.
No table of contents.
      This is an effort to make a mid-decade census (1965)
estimate on Mexican Americans in Houston.   Very brief but

very informative with 12 tables of statistics. Unfortunately
this study is of course dated now. It usually shows the Mexican American lagging behind the Anglo in many of the above
aspects and occasionally behind the Black. Apparently this is
one part of a four-part study on the Mexican American in
Houston.

121   Gorden, Raymond L. Spanish Personal Names as Bar-
      riers to Communication between Latin Americans and
      North Americans. Yellowsprings, Ohio: Antioch Col-
      lege, 1968. 142p.
      Intended to show "how the cultural dissonance between
the Anglo American and the Latin American naming systems
interferes with cross-cultural communication," and is designed "in analyzing over 1, 700, 000 Latin American names
to develop priority lists according to relative popularity and
geographic location in Latin America." Full name versus
nombre completo, the nombre completo in the kinship system,
and alphabetization of the Spanish personal name. Also appendixes on popular names, male and female names, and
priority lists of apellidos for the major Latin American cities.
      This work complements Tibón and the others which
describe the origin of Spanish family names. Gorden is more
interested in describing the structure of Spanish surnames
and given names and the frequency of occurrence of certain
names. The Chicano can find much that is useful here--a
cultural identity with all of Spanish America where his surname probably occurs and an analysis of a naming system
which probably is still operative in Chicano naming.

122   Gosnell, Charles Francis. Spanish Personal Names:
      Principles Governing Their Formation and Use Which
      May Be Presented as a Help for Catalogers and Bib-
      liographers. New York: H. W. Wilson, 1938. 112p.
      This study of value to anyone interested in the rules
governing the origin and usage of Spanish personal names.
Besides the principles in the formation of names, the author
includes chapters on present problems of cataloging of Spanish surnames and sources for verification. The work is divided into five general chapters, a conclusion, and four appendices. Also an 11-page bibliography of reference works
is pertinent to this topic. Has indexes to names used as
examples in the text and subject index.
      The value of this work for Mexican-Americans lies in
chapter IV on formation of names including ancient and medi-

eval history, modern usage, and laws.   The name index and
bibliography are both extremely useful also.   The work's
subtitle falsely limits its usefulness.

123   Gregory, Winifred (ed.).   American Newspapers, 1821-
      1936: A Union List of Files Available in the United
      States and Canada.   New York: H. W. Wilson, 1937.
      791p.
      Lists files available in the U. S. and Canada from the
years suggested in the title.   States are alphabetized as are
the cities listed under them.   The newspapers are arranged
alphabetically under the city.   Information succinct but invaluable: name of newspaper, dates of publication, name changes
and reincorporations, names of depositories and the extent of
their holdings.   For example, "La Prensa," one of the longest runs of a Spanish-language newspaper in the Southwest,
is entered under San Antonio, Texas, as starting February
13, 1913 and following are listed the abbreviations of five depositories and their holdings.   In genealogical studies the
searcher can look up the appropriate city in one of the states
of Chicano concentration and perhaps find a newspaper that
coincides with his ancestor's residence and death.   In this
newspaper it is possible to find such genealogical information
as obituaries, marriages, births, etc.

124   Griffin, Louise (comp.).   Multi-Ethnic Books for Young
      Children: Annotated Bibliography for Parents and
      Teachers.   Washington, D. C. : National Association
      for the Education of Young Children, 1974?
      A guide to children's books that will correspond to the
child's ethnic background.   Eight different ethnic groups including those of Latin American derivation.   Also has section
on adult books for parents and teachers and a directory of
publishers.   No index.
      Two sections of this bibliography relate to the Mexi-
can American--the chapter entitled, "Accent on Latin-Ameri-
can Derivation, " and "Adult Books for Parents and Teachers. "
The latter chapter is the more useful in that it provides a
general list of books regarding children's literature.   The
"Latin American Derivation" has 130 annotated titles on books
in English and Spanish.   Unfortunately these works do not
deal specifically with Mexican-American subjects but with
themes from other Latin cultures.   The author included Mexican but not Mexican American.   The books in Spanish might
be useful for the bilingual child.   In other words, this bibli-

ography contains materials somewhat peripheral but still relevant to the Chicano.

125 Gudde, Erwin G. California Place Names. Los Ange-
        les: University of California Press, 1969. 416p.
      Presents the origin and meaning of place names and
brings out the history of California through the stories of
these names. Covers cities, railway stations, lakes and
rivers, mountain ranges, hills, capes, and islands in a dictionary arrangement. Out of 15,000 place names, the author
has selected the most important and interesting ones. Does
not include vanished names.
      Contains innumerable Spanish place names. Length of
entries varies. In deference to local custom the author gives
English pronunciation, definition as a geographical entity, history of origin of names, and sources of information. Excellent and easy to use and has glossary and bibliography.

126 Gutiérrez, José Angel. A Gringo Manual on How to
        Handle Mexican Americans. Crystal City, Texas:
        Winterside Publishing House, 1974? 185p.
      A guide to alert the Chicano to the tricks and manipu-
lations of the Gringo. Covers nine categories of tricks, plus
one section labeled miscellaneous. Divided into ten categories
and each category with appropriate paragraph numbers.
      The categories include demonstrations, education, foun-
dation, jobs, law and order, media, negotiation, political,
pilón and miscellaneous. Highly readable protest manual.
Bilingual edition.

127 Hackett, Charles Wilson. Historical Documents Relat-
        ing to New Mexico, Nueva Vizcaya, and Approaches
        Thereto to 1773. Washington, D.C.: Carnegie Insti-
        tution, 1923-1937. 3 vols.
      Designed to collect and to publish in English and Span-
ish documents, running from ca. 1590 to 1773, from the Archives of Seville and Mexico City that relate to New Mexico
and Nueva Vizcaya. Volumes I and II relate mainly to New
Mexico while Volume III is Nueva Vizcaya. Each has detailed
table of contents and index.
      Bilingual edition; contains documents definitely relat-
ing to New Mexico. In index are also peripheral references
to Texas and California. Easy to use because of index.

128 Hamilton, Don.   Evaluation Instruments for Bilingual
     Education.   A Revision of Tests in Use in Title VII
     Bilingual Education Projects.   Austin, Texas: Educa-
     tion Service Center 13, 1972.   95p.   ED 087 818
     A bibliography of approximately 221 tests that can be
used for bilingual bicultural education projects.   Each test
described by: title, author, publisher, source, date, pages,
price, age, grade, time, language group or individual, skills,
special requirements and scores.   Although high school included, the tests seem to be mainly for elementary and
junior high.
     It would appear that all disciplines are covered in the
various exams listed, but verbal skills seem to be empha-
sized.   The titles and sources of these tests suggest that bi-
lingual/bicultural here refers to Spanish-speaking persons in
the United States.   Index makes this work easy to use.   Valuable bibliography for educators in bilingual/bicultural studies.
Could supplement the work of Pamela Rosen (q. v.).

129 Hanna, Phil Townsend.   California: Through Five Cen-
     turies; A Handbook of Memorable Historical Dates.
     New York: Farrar and Rinehart, 1935.   212p.
     Traces "the development of California from its earli-
est recorded historical annals to the present time. "   The
earliest entry is 1540 and the latest is 1935.   Limited to
California and its Anglo/Spanish background.   All entries
are chronological but Hanna has divided the book into seven
sections: conquistadores (1540-1822); liberty, fraternity,
equality (1822-1846); Manifest Destiny (1846-1848); argonauts
(1848-1869); iron horses (1869-1885); growth and the soil
(1885-1900); and turning the century (1900-1935).   Table of
contents and subject index.
     Approximately 760 entries.   Each with precise date
and a paragraph of description of the significance of the event
on that date.   Many of the entries in the index suggest a
Spanish or Mexican American topic: discovery, government,
missions, Catholic padres, Franciscans, and innumerable
Spanish surnames.   This reference work is a type of "who
was who" in California history.   This work also has much
that is Anglo or non-Mexican but it is of value for quick reference in the Spanish background of California.

130 Harrigan, Joan (comp.).   Materials tocante los latinos:
     A Bibliography of Materials on the Spanish Americans.
     Denver: Colorado Department of Education, 1967.   36p.

A multipurpose bibliography that provides more understanding of Spanish-named people: Cuban, Puerto Rican,
Spanish, and Mexican. All genres included but only in books.
Contains a general reading list, young adult, elementary,
dual language edition, bibliographies and professional materials. No index or table of contents.

The scope is too general to make this work very useful. Selection seems to be based on a sampling of all types
of material from the Spanish world and the Southwest. The
arrangement is chaotic. See next entry.

131   Harrigan, Joan (comp.). More materials tocante los
      latinos: A Bibliography of Materials on the Spanish-
      Americans. Denver: Colorado Department of Educa-
      tion, 1969. 28p.
      Supplements the 1967 bibliography (see previous entry)
on a similar topic. Makes a broad appeal. Students of all
ages, materials for education and libraries, ERIC materials
and new and forthcoming materials, arranged in this order.
      Approximately 125 briefly annotated entries. Guide-
lines for inclusion of materials very broad. Diverse topics
such as Mexico, bibliography for teachers of linguistically
handicapped, adult education, etc. In spite of the title, many
of the entries refer to the Mexican American.

132   Harrigan, Joan (comp.). Tesoro de oro; Books for
      Spanish Speaking Students. Denver: Colorado State
      Library, 1966. 11p.
      Intended "to provide lists of our bilingual materials
available and of sources for all types of materials for re-in-
forcing the cultural heritage of our Spanish-American com-
patriots. " Bilingual books for elementary students, separate
editions for elementary students, bilingual books for older
readers, list and sources of materials for older readers,
periodicals, directory of sources.
      Contains 56 unevaluated entries. In addition to normal
bibliographical information, also gives age level. This work
is comparatively early and not as useful therefore as Nichols'
Multicultural Bibliography for Preschool... (q. v.). Of most
value are the six criteria for judging bilingual books. The
books listed in this bibliography do not necessarily have a
Mexican-American theme.

133   Harris, Alice A. Había una vez: A Selected Bibliogra-

phy of Children's Books.   Oakland, Cal.:   Latin American Library, 1968.   40p.
Identifies the best literature in Spanish for children in
the Oakland Public Library.   Author annotates approximately
222 titles for readers from kindergarten through junior high;
arranged alphabetically by author.
Each title is evaluated according to difficulty.   Plot
summary plus mention of illustrations, format and binding.
Many titles are in Spanish but author indicates when text is
in English.

134 Hayes-Bautista, David E., and Eleanor Moreno Kent
     (comps.).   A Resource List of Mexican-American Or-
     ganizations and Services in the East Bay.   Oakland,
     Cal.:   Latin American Library, n.d.   40p.
References to resources available for Mexican Americans in the East Bay area.   Lists national and state organizations, service centers, local organizations, organizations un-
contacted, agencies with services in Spanish and churches;
arranged in this order but as divided into two parts--Alameda
County and Contra Costa County.   Has table of contents and
index to organizations.
An invaluable guide for Mexican Americans in this
area who need certain types of services pertinent to their
ethnic group.   Gives name of organization, at times gives
purpose, officers, and addresses.   Has also the main national organizations.   Excellent index makes this very easy
to use.

135 Haywood, Charles.   A Bibliography of North American
     Folklore and Folksong.   V. I The American People
     North of Mexico, Including Canada.   V. II The Amer-
     ican Indians North of Mexico Including the Eskimos.
     New York: Dover Publications, 1961.   2 vols.
A compilation of folklore of the U.S., apparently limited mainly to printed materials and some records.   Volume I
arranged by general bibliography, regional bibliography, ethnic bibliography, occupational and miscellaneous.   Table of
contents but no index.
Three sections of this work relate specifically to the
Mexican American--the Southwest, the West, and ethnic bibliography.   Approximately 43 pages of unannotated entries on
Mexican Americans.   Has general studies, folktales, customs,
beliefs, superstitions, folk medicine, proverbs, speech and
place names.   Volume I will be the most useful; however,

volume II on Indians might list works that relate the Indian
to the Spaniard.

136   Heathman, James E. (comp.). Migrant Education: A
      Selected Bibliography. Las Cruces, N. M. : Educa-
      tional Resources Information Center Clearinghouse on
      Rural Education and Small Schools, 1969. 41p.
      ----. ---- Supplement. 1970. 41p.
          Provides access to materials on latest developments
in the education of migrant children. Limited to this specific topic. Includes documents from ERIC, Office of Education Research Reports and Research in Education. Entries
are by document number; consequently it is unalphabetical.
However, a subject index with 48 subdivisions provides access
by document number.
          Each entry is abstracted sufficiently to preclude read-
ing. Here migrant can be interpreted as anyone in this category, not only Mexican-American. In 1970 this volume was
updated with a 41-page supplement with a similar format.

137   Heathman, James E. , and Cecilia J. Martinez. Mexi-
      can American Education; A Selected Bibliography.
      Las Cruces, N. M. : New Mexico State University,
      ERIC/CRESS, 1969. 56p.
          Produced in order to cite research findings on educa-
tion of the Mexican American that appeared in Research in
Education. Contains all pertinent documents from Research
in Education from November 1967 to June 1969, arranged by
ERIC code number. User must first refer to subject index
to find pertinent article.
          Approximately 48 entries, with code number, title,
author, price, length, and brief descriptive annotation. Mul-
titopic coverage of all aspects of education relating to the
Mexican American. Most entries refer to elementary and
secondary education. For a more thorough coverage with a
similar format, see Edgar B. Charles.

138   Hester, Golda (comp.). A Select Bibliography on Mexi-
      can Americans. Austin, Texas: Hispanic American
      Institute, 1972. 8p.
          Presents a cross section of the Mexican-American
materials in the University of Texas at Austin libraries.
Only monographs that are examples of all aspects of Mexican Americans from all disciplines. Arranged alphabetically

by author in one integrated list. However, the last two
pages list separately bibliographies and some significant periodicals.
     Approximately 128 unannotated entries. Naturally this
is only a sample of the holdings of the University of Texas
libraries on Mexican Americans. It is meant for the gen-
eralist as it lists pertinent monographs from all disciplines
that relate to Mexican Americans. This could serve as a
guideline for a core collection on Mexican Americans. However, the specialist would probably want to refer to the bibliographies listed.

139 Historical Records Survey. Arizona. The 1864 Census
     of the Territory of Arizona. Phoenix: The Survey,
     1938. 210p.
     The first publication of the census of the territory of
Arizona for three judicial districts or the state.
     On each person enumerated, the following information
is available--age, sex, marital status, birthplace, how long
resident, when naturalized, if not naturalized by what right
claims citizenship, area of residence, occupation, value of
real estate and personal estate. Many Mexicans in this survey, for one of its purposes was to determine the intentions
of the Mexicans who could make a choice of citizenship according to the eighth article of the Treaty of Guadalupe Hidalgo.

140 Historical Records Survey. California. Guide to De-
     positories of Manuscript Collections in the United
     States: California. Los Angeles: Southern California
     Historical Records Survey Project, 1941. 76p.
     Presents the history, collection policies, nature, size
and condition of manuscript holdings of 74 California depositories. Mainly manuscript collections of public libraries,
universities, museums, and missions of California. Lacking
are state and county and city archives. Arranged alphabetically by geographical location. Table of contents and index to
names of collections. Also subject index.
     Guide to 74 manuscript collections in California. Al-
though much is definitely not Mexican American, much could
be considered pertinent to la raza--the collection of the genealogical society, mission archives indicating baptisms, the
holdings of the Bancroft Library on early Californiana; much
in the Los Angeles County Museum of History relates to the
same subject. The holdings seem to be mainly 19th century.

Selectively they could be a resource for studies of the Mexican American.

141 Historical Records Survey. Colorado. Guide to Vital
     Statistics Records in Colorado. Vol. 2, Church Ar-
     chives. Denver: Colorado Historical Records Survey,
     1942. 166p.
        Presents an accurate guide to vital statistics records,
from approximately 1850 to ca. 1940, in church depositories
in Colorado. Covers Protestant and Catholic churches.
Churches entered alphabetically under county, then city; e. g. ,
Archuleta County, Pagosa Springs, Seventh Day Adventist
Church. No index.
        Unless absorbed by a later study this must be one of
the most complete guides to church archives in Colorado.
Mentions that church records sometimes preceded civil records. Consequently, this might be the only source for some
records. Ethnic congregations not noted but occasionally a
church will bear a label such as Spanish Methodist or San
Isidro Catholic. Each entry specifies denomination, date of
founding, address, and brief summary of contents of register.

142 Historical Records Survey. New Mexico. Guide to
     Public Vital Statistics in New Mexico. Albuquerque:
     New Mexico Historical Records Survey, 1942. 135p.
        Finding guide to the vital statistics records, 17th cen-
tury to ca. 1940, of New Mexico. Births, deaths, marriages,
divorces, and church records, arranged in this order. Also
an index to births, deaths, and marriages by counties and a
subject index.
        In addition to information on availability of records,
this work also has some short explanatory pages about public
records in New Mexico. Records are entered by county;
under county, records are given by dates. Gives brief information on how surnames were entered. Very easy to use.
Naturally many of the records will refer to Mexican Americans.

143 Historical Records Survey. Works Program Adminis-
     tration. Inventory of County Archives of Arizona,
     1938; Inventory of County Archives of California, 1937;
     Inventory of County Archives of Colorado; Inventory of
     County Archives of New Mexico, 1938; and Inventory
     of County Archives of Texas, 1942.

This work is an "attempt further to sketch in the historical background of the county or other unit of government, and to describe precisely and in detail the organization and functions of the government agencies whose records they list. The county, town, and other local inventories for the entire county, will, when completed, constitute an encyclopedia of local government, as well as a bibliography of local archives." The above titles refer to many volumes. Each state attempted a separate volume for each of its counties. An outline of the functions of all county offices and a description of the types of records maintained. All county inventories follow a similar format--county and its records system, and county offices and their records. In the latter are included commissioners court, county clerk, district court, county court, justice of peace court, grand jury, county attorney, sheriff, constable, tax assessor-collector, board of equalization, county treasurer, county board of school trustees, county school superintendent, county surveyor and public weigher. Bibliography, chronological index and subject and entry index.

This series would comprise many volumes from each state. Although Mexican Americans are not identified in the subject index, they doubtlessly figure in innumerable documents in these Southwestern states. For example, some of the more general headings that would incorporate Mexican American would be: marriages, deaths, naturalization, etc. An invaluable resource for many types of social science or genealogical research. These same inventories possibly exist for counties in states other than the Southwest.

144 Hopper, Jean. The Migratory Farm Worker: A Selected Bibliography. Philadelphia: Free Library of Philadelphia, 1967. 8p.

A guide to materials relating to migratory farm workers in the Free Library of Philadelphia. Print and non-print materials--monographs, pamphlets, government publications, periodical articles, sources of information, and 16mm films.

Short bibliography of highly useful works on a specialized subject within Mexican-American studies, i.e., the migratory farm worker. Many of the unannotated entries refer to the Mexican American or are background studies on agricultural migrants. This bibliography also has fictional works on migrants such as Steinbeck's In Dubious Battle. Approximately 12 annotated entries on films. Sources of information here refers to organizations interested in migrant labor. Missing are bibliographies, indexes and abstracts. Though now dated, presents a good cross-section of the subject.

145 Huerta, Jorge A. (ed.). A Bibliography of Chicano and
     Mexican Dance, Drama and Music. Oxnard, Cal.:
     Colegio Quetzalcoatl, 1972. 59p.
     Mainly provides a reference source for these perform-
ing arts among the Chicano, from books, journals, plays,
and phonograph records. Arranged first by creative art,
then by chronology, then format. In other words, dance is
presented in the pre-Columbian period in books and journals;
then in Mexico in books and journals; finally in Aztlán in
books and journals. No index but table of contents.
     Approximately 700 unannotated entries. Of these, 114
are Chicano. The editor availed himself of ten main sources
in his search for these entries. No theses or dissertations
mentioned. One of the few reference sources on Chicano
creative arts.

146 Illinois. Commission on Human Relations. Education
     Services Department. Bibliography on Hispano Amer-
     ica: History and Culture. n. p., 1972. 32p.
     "An attempt to create a bridge of communication for
Hispano America." General history and culture of Hispano
America, Puerto Ricans, Chicanos and resources, and story
books for children. All print materials and all topics in
both English and Spanish. Has table of contents but no index.
     Apparently Hispano America is broadly interpreted as
meaning all of Spanish America and Spanish Americans living
in the United States. The guidelines are so broad as to be
non-existent. To include in 32 pages even a good cross-section on the above mentioned themes would be difficult. The
section on Chicanos has only eight works listed that actually
relate to this ethnic group. It is difficult to determine any
public for whom this bibliography would be useful.

147 Indiana University at Bloomington. The Libraries.
     Mexican Americans [xeroxed]. Bloomington, Ind.,
     1972. ----. ---- Supplement, 1973. 25p.
     A xeroxed guide to Mexican-American materials in the
Indiana University libraries. Mainly monographs with entries generally on Mexican Americans; some on minorities in
general in the United States; others on Mexican works. Organized alphabetically by main entry.
     400 unannotated entries to the Mexican-American hold-
ings. Only monographs mentioned. No criteria given as to
selection.

148   Institute for Rural America.   Poverty, Rural Poverty
      and Minority Groups Living in Rural Poverty: An An-
      notated Bibliography.   Lexington, Ky.:   Spindletop Re-
      search, 1969.   159p.
      "A selective and representative compilation of avail-
able resources on a wide-ranging array of categories under
general poverty, rural poverty, and those minority groups
most closely associated with poverty." Arranged into the following broad topics: poverty in the United States, rural
poverty, and minority groups living in rural poverty.   No index but detailed table of contents, i. e. , each of the broad
divisions mentioned refined into numerous subtopics.
      Approximately 1000 descriptively annotated entries of
monographs, government documents, and articles.   Two sections relate specifically to the Mexican-Americans: migrants
in rural poverty and Spanish Americans in rural poverty.
The latter is subdivided into: social, economic, and demographic characteristics; discrimination; labor patterns; legislation; and land reform.   Three other divisions are peripheral
to the Chicano: poverty in the U. S. , rural poverty, and the
aged in rural poverty.   This is an excellent bibliography for
the broad context that it provides the user and for its 14 subdivisions that relate directly to Chicanos.

149   Institute of Texan Cultures.   The Mexican Texans.   San
      Antonio: The Institute, 1971.   32p.
      Biographical sketches of Mexicans in Texas, 1709-
1971.   Entries are chronological; no index or table of contents.
      48 uncritical biographical sketches of 150 words in
length, accompanied by pictures, that give basic information
and achievements.   Probably best for junior high and high
school because of text and illustrations.   No bibliographies
included.   Title allows compiler to incorporate figures prior
to Mexican or Texas independence.

150   Instituto Chicano de Artes y Artesanias (comp.).   Chi-
      cano Art of the Southwest: Color Slide Collection
      [technical unit].   2 vols.   San Antonio, Texas: The
      Institute, 1974.
      Intended to present a cross section of Chicano visual
art through slides and to introduce Chicano artists through
brief biographical paragraphs.   Approximately 220 colored
slides of paintings, drawings, sculptures, graphics, murals,
and posters.   The collection is arranged in two volumes.

Each is a notebook that contains approximately 100 slides in
transparent plastic and eight pages of descriptions and biographical sketches. This is an extremely valuable reference
tool because along with the study of Jactino Quirarte, Mexican American Artists, it is probably the only book-length
guide to Chicano art.

This collection has a great advantage--its flexibility
for the various colored slides can be removed for individual
study. Its orientation is mainly contemporary Chicano art
and themes that are identifiably Chicano. Hopefully a later
work with a similar format will include the santero art of
New Mexico. The second half is a type of biographical reference to 30 Mexican American artists from the Southwest.
Copy evaluated was obtained at the Latin American Collection
at the University of Texas in Austin.

151   Jablonsky, Adelaide (comp.).   Mexican Americans: An
      Annotated Bibliography of Doctoral Dissertations.
      ERIC-IRCD Doctoral Research Series, no. 1, May
      1973. New York: Columbia University, ERIC Clear-
      ing House on the Urban Disadvantaged, 1973. 88p.
      ED 076 714
      Guide to dissertations in education concerning the Mex-
ican American. Covers ca. 1965 to 1973 research on academic achievement, bilingual education, disadvantaged youth, economically disadvantaged, school integration, etc. Citations
are entered alphabetically by author surname under the following topics: bilingual, verbal, reading, self-concept, cultural, parental influence, comparison with other groups, Jen-
sen Theory, and mathematics. Has subject, author and insti-
tutional indexes.

Has 62 entries of abstract length on education of Mexican Americans treated in dissertations. These entries were
culled from Dissertations Abstracts and university libraries.
One of the purposes of this bibliography was to diffuse information on research that is often lost, i. e. , the dissertation. Invaluable as a guideline to semicurrent research on
Mexican Americans and education. According to the preface,
700 titles were found and the others will be placed in bibliographic form later.

152   January, William Spence Jr.   The Chicano Dialect of
      the Mexican American Communities of Dallas and Fort
      Worth.   M. A. thesis.   Fort Worth: Texas Christian
      University, 1970.

January attempts to determine if the words from the Colthrop study of El Paso are also known in Dallas and Fort Worth. His study seems thorough for he includes historical background, bilingualism of Mexican Americans in these two cities, dialectology, methods, Chicano vocabulary, taboo vocabulary, dialect of the Chicano underground, and distribution by age group. The author orients the reader to the methodology and the purpose of his work and it is one of the few studies on Chicano vocabulary that results from scientific rigor. Two separate Chicano dictionaries are incorporated. In the more important one, Chicano vocabulary, he alphabetizes 412 words arranging them according to: part of speech, area where encountered, authoritative dictionaries in which the word is not present, age group of the informants, a number-letter coding that describes the informant as to area and occupation; and finally the definition. He has 98 entries from the dialect of the Chicano underground.

January's thesis, although well researched and superior to most studies of this nature, unfortunately has not been published. The copy evaluated was obtained from the library at Texas Christian University.

153   Johnson, Ronald.   The Aficionado's Southwestern Cooking.   Albuquerque: University of New Mexico Press, 1968.   124p.
Presents and adapts Mexican food to U.S. kitchens and palates. Basic Mexican dishes plus short section on ingredients and methods. Recipes listed under separate categories, i.e., meats, eggs, etc. Table of contents and index.
Approximately 150 recipes. Mainly Mexican recipes adapted to the U.S. that do not become more narrowly regional than Southwestern. Recipes somehow seem more Americanized than those of the other cookbooks mentioned.

154   Jones, Lamar Babington.   Mexican-American Labor Problems in Texas.   Ph.d. dissertation.   Austin: University of Texas, 1965.   234p.
Designed "to chart the course national manpower policy has taken among the Mexican-American workers in the Texas border area...." Covers 1901 to 1963. As stated in title, concentrates mainly on border area and specifically on Laredo and El Paso. Mostly agriculture and border cities type of employment. Five chapters--immigration history, alien commuters, farm labor, economic insecurity of Texas Mexican American farm laborers and summary and conclusions.

Has 28 tables plus an appendix.

This dissertation has value in that it concentrates on the labor problems of the Texas border and summarizes much data in 28 charts presenting statistics. In his bibliography Jones suggests reliance on information from various sources: government publications, the State of Texas, legal items, etc. Could be used with the Schmidt work.

155 Jones, Robert C. Mexicans in the United States; A Bibliography. Washington, D. C. : Pan American Union, 1942. 14p.

A bibliography intended to supplement Emory S. Bogardus' work (q. v.). Books and magazine articles from ca. 1916 to ca. 1940. General references, urban settlements and industrial labor, agricultural labor, fiction, and social problems, arranged in that order. Brevity precludes need for table of contents or index.

Approximately 225 unannotated entries. Surely not to be used as a first source because these entries have probably been incorporated into a later bibliography. Interesting as an example of state of the art of Mexican American bibliography in 1942. This 1942 work was reprinted by Arno Press in 1974 and incorporated into Mexican American Bibliographies, edited by Carlos E. Cortes.

156 Jones, Robert C. Selected References on the Labor Importation Program between Mexico and the United States. Washington, D. C. : Pan American Union, 1948. 5p.

Mainly 1918-1946 magazine and journal articles and government publications from the United States; nine entries in Spanish give Mexican point of view on this topic. Arranged in five parts--general aspects; agricultural labor; railroad labor; agreements; decrees and laws; and Mexican sources.

Approximately 65 unannotated articles comprise this specialized bibliography. Brevity precludes need for index.

157 Jordan, Lois B. Mexican Americans: Resources to Build Cultural Understanding. Littleton, Col. : Libraries Unlimited, 1973. 265p.

Bibliography for the young of Mexican American materials in all forms, genres, and time periods. Has two main sections--printed materials and audiovisual materials.

The former is subdivided: Mexico's history, Mexican Americans in the United States, the arts, literature, biography
and fiction. Well indexed by topic and author.
  1028 entries with brief descriptive annotations. Makes
no distinction between Mexican and Chicano and the sociological section is not delimited. Main weakness is inability to
establish criteria as to inclusion of materials.

158 Jorgensen, Venita. <u>Guide to Materials on Mexican</u>
   <u>Americans in the University of California at Riverside</u>
   <u>Library</u> [mimeographed]. Riverside, Cal., 1970. 18p.
   Guide to monographs and government documents.
Three main categories--Mexican Americans, works on sociology, and Mexico. List of newspapers also.
  Approximately 216 unannotated entries. Lacks periodical articles or films and there are no discernible guidelines as to inclusion.

159 Juárez-Lincoln Center (comp.). <u>Nuestra Comunidad:</u>
   <u>A Directory of Chicano, Latin American, and Span-</u>
   <u>ish-Speaking Groups.</u> Austin: Juarez Lincoln Center,
   <u>1973?</u> unpaged.
   Guide to the 30 groups in Austin, Texas, which work
with Mexican-Americans. Arranged alphabetically by group.
  Each organization has address, contact person,
phone(s), meeting place, time and dates, and statement of
purpose. Lists variety of organizations from musical groups
to charitable groups.

160 Keating, Charlotte Matthews. <u>Building Bridges of Un-</u>
   <u>derstanding.</u> Tucson: Palo Verde Pub. Co., 1967.
   <u>134p.</u>
  A guide to reading materials for children from non-
English-speaking homes--i.e., American Indian, Spanish-
speaking ethnic groups, Japanese Americans, and other
minorities. Each minority group section is divided into three parts--pre-school and primary levels, upper elementary, and junior high and high school. Author and subject index.
  The Spanish-speaking covered in 20 pages; 22 books
evaluated with plot summaries and age level appreciation.
Stories about Mexicans seem to predominate.

161   Kelley, Victor Harold.   The Teaching of the Spanish-
        Speaking Child.   Tucson: University of Arizona Li-
        brary, ca. 1939.   6p.
        A partial holdings list on this subject in the University
of Arizona library.   Monographs and journal articles (integrated) and University of Arizona theses (listed separately),
all from the 1930's.
        Approximately 100 unannotated entries that deal spe-
cifically with teaching methods and Mexican and Mexican-
American culture.   The list now is extremely dated and lacks
an introduction on guidelines for selection.   Main value today is as an early example of interest in a problem which
is only now receiving concerted attention.

162   Kelly, George W. , and Rex R. Kelly.   Farm and Ranch
        Spanish.   Kerville, Texas: Braswell Printing Co. ,
        1971.   241p.
        Covers vocabulary and phrases for basic farm Span-
ish for Anglo ranchers and farmers.   Divided into three sec-
tions--ranch, farm, and grammar.   Two short dictionaries:
Spanish/English and English/Spanish.
        Very practical approach to Spanish with 27 chapters
on such topics as house cleaning, care of vehicle, yard work,
etc.   Most of the Spanish vocabulary included is used in the
farming districts of Texas.   Bilingual dictionary at end gives
only definitions.

163   Kelly, George W. and Rex R. Kelly.   Spanish for the
        Housewife.   Kerville, Texas: Braswell Printing Co. ,
        1973.   163p.
        According to the authors, this work is "to assist in
the everyday activities of homes, many of which employ
Spanish-speaking people part or all of the time. "   As implied
by its title, it limits itself to the vocabulary, phrases, and
sentences necessary for the English-speaking employers of
Spanish kitchen help.   The work is divided into 25 short chapters mainly devoted to the various divisions of household activities: the kitchen, bedrooms, washing clothes, the table,
etc.   The longest chapter relates to grammar.   The final two
chapters are Spanish-English and English-Spanish vocabularies.
Apparently this work had its genesis in Farm and Ranch Spanish, an initial compilation by the same two authors in 1961.
Naturally Spanish for the Housewife is designed for the mono-
lingual Anglo who employs Mexican Americans and as such
would not be a reference work of much aid to the Spanish-

speaking Chicano.   The Spanish-English vocabulary has approximately 900 entries with only the English equivalent.
Apparently the words were compiled from observation of Mexican Americans.   Yet no methodology is suggested in the
preface and the authors used no written sources for they con-
fess: ''Hence there can be no bibliography for this text.   The
only bibliography is the Mexican people themselves, Mexicans of all classes. ''   A glance at the Spanish-English vocabulary list suggests that the words and definitions could be
found in any standard dictionary.   In the section on grammar,
there is nothing on the subjunctive or the imperative.   Spanish for the Housewife is valuable for the dilettante who needs
some basic working vocabulary; for the scholar interested in
Texas Spanish, the Dictionary of the Spanish of Texas by Galvan and Teschner is recommended.

164   Kelly, Rex Robert.   Vocabulary as Used on the Mexican
      Border.   Master's Thesis, Baylor University.   Waco,
      Texas, 1938.   39p.
      To select the special words used in the Spanish lan-
guage on the Texas-Mexican border.   ''Special'' here means
words not found in any standard dictionary of Spanish.   Arranged by categories: animals, foods, people, underworld
terms, sporting terms, automobile terms, miscellaneous
words, and modismos.
      Approximately 420 words with spelling and definition,
but without pronunciation or use in a sentence.   Occasionally
gives etymology of words.

165   Kercheville, F. M.   A Preliminary Glossary of New
      Mexico Spanish.   Albuquerque: University of New
      Mexico Press, 1934.   (University of New Mexico Bul-
      letin, Language Series, vol. 5.)   68p.
      Preliminary study to aid students who wish to gather
data for a final study.   Covers Spanish in New Mexican newspapers and in conversation from the year 1934.   No mention
of geographical area of concentration within New Mexico.
Divided into six parts.   I. Colloquialisms, II. Words which
suffer phonetic changes, III. Archaic or obsolete words, IV.
Words of Indian origin, V. Mexicanisms used in New Mexico,
and VI. Hispanicized English words and expressions.
      Gives Spanish word with English equivalent--and no
other information.   Compilers attempted to select only the
words that have unique use in New Mexico.   Very small dictionary but apparently one of the earliest.

166   Kielman, Chester Valls.   The University of Texas Archives: A Guide to the Historical Manuscript Collections in the University of Texas Library.   Austin:
University of Texas Press, 1967.   594p.
Guide to 2430 collections at the University of Texas.
Works date from 16th century but mainly are 19th and 20th
century.   Arranged alphabetically by collection.   Has a topical and name index.
     Each entry has dates delimiting time scope of contents,
a short paragraph describing formats and themes within each
collection, and a note as to size.   Innumerable entries appear to be relevant to Mexican Americans.

167   Kinton, Jack F.   American Ethnic Groups and the Re-
vival of Cultural Pluralism: Evaluative Sourcebook
for the 1970's.   Aurora.   Ill. :   Social Science and
Sociological Recources, 1974.   205p.
     Guide to print and non-print resources of American
ethnic groups.   Ethnic group theory, ethnic and quasi-ethnic
groups, America's immigrant and emigrant, race relations,
and Black Americans, filmography, and directory of research
and cultural centers.   Arranged in the above order with entry by author surname.   No index but detailed table of contents.   The Mexican American here is given only 12 pages
of unannotated entries as he is included with 25 other ethnic
groups.
     The monographs and articles in this section on the
Chicano are standard entries in most bibliographies.   The
value then of this work is the context in which it places the
Mexican American for here are three sections that normally
are not included in Chicano bibliography: ethnic group theory
and America, immigrants, and emigrants provide excellent
background for study of the Mexican American.   Also Kinton
provides a directory of research centers on Chicanos.   Of
similar value is the section on filmography that incorporates
Mexican Americans and the topics of immigration and integration.   Copy evaluated seen at Trinity University in San Antonio, Texas.

168   Kolm, Richard (comp.).   Bibliography of Ethnicity and
Ethnic Groups.   Rockville, Md. :   National Institute of
Mental Health, 1973.   250p.
     A bibliography intended "to explore the theory and the
social, cultural and psychological consequences of membership in a minority or ethnic group. "   "Minority group" in this

bibliography is an inclusive term--Negro, Indian, Mexican
American, Oriental, Scandinavian, etc. Also includes assimilation, intermarriage, and other topics that relate to
minority groups in the monographs and journal articles only.
Divided into two sections--annotated and unannotated. Subject
index leads to numbered paragraphs.
451 annotated entries and 1193 unannotated entries.
At least 108 of the entries refer to Mexican Americans.
Most of these references can be found in standard bibliographies of Mexican Americans. The value of this work lies
in the broad references that relate to all minorities in the
U. S. , e. g. , acculturation, adjustment, bilingualism, education, etc. All entries from the library of the Catholic University of America and the Library of Congress.

169 Landolt, Robert Garland. The Mexican American Work-
     ers of San Antonio, Texas. Ph. D. dissertation. Aus-
     tin: University of Texas, 1965. 379p.
     Designed "to determine the nature and extent of the
utilization of the Mexican American segment of the labor
force in San Antonio ... and to examine the probable causes
of ethnic imbalances in employment and income...." Although the study is relatively recent, statistics go back to
1820. Ethnic heritage, 20th-century population movements,
employment and income of labor force, military, organized
labor and the construction industry, manufacturing industry,
nonmanufacturing, politics, education, hiring, and cultural
inhibitions and social barriers are all covered, arranged in
that order. Table of contents and guide to table and maps.
     Probably the only detailed study of the Mexican Amer-
ican population of San Antonio. This work has reference
value because of its scope and thoroughness. Author sub-
stantiates thesis with 48 statistical tables and three maps and
a seven-page bibliography. This work is invaluable to understanding the Mexican American in San Antonio. Available on
microfilm.

170 Layer, Harold A. Ethnic Studies and Audio Visual
     Media: A Listing and Discussion. Stanford, Cal. :
     Stanford University: ERIC Clearinghouse on Educa-
     tional Media and Technology, 1969. ED 031 091
     List of audio tapes, 16mm films, filmstrips, record-
ings, videotapes, and transparencies on non white minorities
in the U. S. Mainly for high school and college. Divided into sections: general ethnic studies, Asian-American studies,

Black studies, Mexican/Spanish American studies and Native
American studies.   Two sections are relevant to the Mexican
American.   General ethnic studies has 36 unannotated entries
which deal with racism, migrant workers, police, welfare,
etc.   Fifteen titles under Mexican/Spanish American studies
mainly relate to the Chicanos.

    This bibliography is now dated but it is the only one
that is specifically on the various non-print media.   With so
few entries, it would have been helpful to annotate them.
Also has two pages of sources for audiovisual media.

171   Lebya, Charles.   A Brief Bibliography on Teacher Edu-
      cation and Chicanos.   Washington, D. C. :   ERIC Clear-
      inghouse on Teacher Education, 1974.   17p.   ED 090
      147
    A guide to monographs, articles, and reports--mainly
from 1968 to 1971--as reported in Research in Education, on
Chicanos and teacher education.   One of the goals of this
bibliography is to "lead to a rethinking of how to provide the
best education possible for Chicano children and youth."   Arranged alphabetically by author surname.   No index.

    25 entries on the above mentioned topic.   Each entry
has author, title, publisher, date of publication, number of
pages, availability and an excellent descriptive abstract.
This is probably the only bibliography that deals with the
specific topic of teacher training and the Chicanos.   Sample
titles: Staff Development of Bilingual Programs, Value Con-
flicts Experienced by Mexican-American Students, In-Service
Teacher Education in a Tri-Ethnic Community: A Partici-
pant Observer Study, etc.

172   Lelevier, Benjamin Jr.   A Portfolio of Outstanding
      Americans of Mexican Descent.   Menlo Park, Cal. :
      Educational Consulting Associates, 1970.   37p.
    "Offer[s] graphically and bilingually a cross section of
Mexican American achievement in our society":   37 biograph-
ical sketches of important Americans of Mexican descent,
arranged alphabetically by surname of person biographized.
In the field of biography more must be done on Mexican
Americans.

    This work, although well illustrated and presenting
Mexican Americans from all over the Southwest and of value
for junior high schools and high schools, suffers from several defects.   All of the Mexican Americans depicted are males
implying a subordinate contribution of the Chicanas.   All are

20th century emphasizing that until now la raza has had few
leaders. All have Spanish surnames and the compiler seems
to ignore the existence of Mexicans with non-Hispanic surnames. The collection is not bound, i. e. , each subject is
on a separate loose sheet. The evaluated copy was obtained
from Trinity University in San Antonio, Texas.

173 Link, Albert D. Mexican American Education: A Se-
     lected Bibliography with ERIC Abstracts. Las Cruces,
     N. M. : ERIC, 1972. (ERIC/CRESS Supple. no. 2.)
     unpaged.
     Provides access to materials that relate broadly to
Mexican American education. Abstracts of ERIC and Current
Index to Journals of Education. Multiple aspects of Mexican
Americans, i. e. , education, migrant workers, health, Spanish surname farm operators, multilingualism. Part II composed of citations from Current Index to Journals in Education and contains entries more peripheral to the Mexican
American such as Spanish American literature, unwed moth-
ers, the bilingually advantaged, etc. Entries in numerical
order according to ERIC numbers. No index.
     As with most ERIC publications this one provides a
brief abstract of articles for the user that enables him to
ascertain usefulness. Also has accession number, publication
date, descriptors, identifier, and price. As suggested above,
this bibliography is mainly on education, but has a variety
of topics. Has 213 well-annotated entries. Main defect is
its generality.

174 Lloyd, Elwood. Arizonology (Knowledge of Arizona).
     Flagstaff, Ariz. : Coconino Sun, 1933. 91p.
     "An easy reference for persons who are interested in
knowing something of the intimate details associated with the
many interesting places named on the recent maps of Arizona. "
Dictionary of place names limited to Arizona. Four classes
--Spanish, Indian, coined, and hybrid.
     Approximately 1272 place names. Each with pronun-
ciation, meaning, location, and other gazetteer type information. Many of the entries naturally are of Spanish origin and
suggest the Spanish heritage of the Mexican American in
Arizona. At times also includes the names of Spanish ex-
plorers. This is an informative, easy-to-use place name dictionary. Author, however, lists no sources or indications of
methodology. He gives the impression of being a self-taught
folklorist. For more detailed information on Arizona and suggested references, see William C. Barnes.

175 López, Lino M. Colorado Latin American Personalities.
Denver: A. M. Printing Co., 1959. 76p.
Biographical sketches of 20th-century leaders of the
Latin American community in Colorado, mainly of New Mexican or Colorado origin, arranged alphabetically.
Approximately 76 single-page biographical sketches of
achievers chosen from all fields. This study has the rather
didactic goal of presenting Mexican Americans who became
successes in their fields in spite of obstacles.

176 Loventhal, Milton, et al. (comp.). Bibliografía de ma-
teriales tocantes al chicano: A Bibliography of Materials Relating to the Chicano in the Library, California State University, San Jose. 2d ed. San Jose:
California State University Library, 1972. 222p.
A guide to materials on Mexico and the Mexican American at the University Library--books, theses, dissertations,
U. S. and California government documents, tapes, records,
microprint materials and periodical titles. Includes only materials on shelf as of 1972. All materials listed under various topics which are alphabetized. Detailed table of contents
and two indexes, author and title.
Approximately 2492 unannotated titles. Most of these
are on Mexico. However, 518 of these are on the Mexican
Americans and arranged under 16 different topics. Aside
from this section, several other sections relate to the Mexican American. These are agricultural laborers by states,
bilingualism, children of migrant laborers, migrant labor and
the new Southwest. As a bibliography of one library's Chicano collection, this is one of the best for its scope, its
highly structured organization and its dual indexing. Also includes creative fiction by Anglo writers. This bibliography
updates Smith (q. v.).

177 Lowery, Woodbury. Descriptive List of Maps of the
Spanish Within the Present Limits of the United States,
1502-1820. Washington, D. C.: GPO, 1912. 567p.
Description of 750 maps in the Library of Congress
pertaining to the Spanish settlements in the United States and
North America as a whole, 1502-1820. Maps are arranged
chronologically then by cartographer's surname. Three in-
dexes: author list, title list, and geographical list.
Of the 750 maps, approximately 350 relate to the
Southwest: 16 on Arizona, 204 on California, 105 on New
Mexico, and 51 on Texas. Each entry has date, cartographer,

brief description of contents of maps, size and sporadically
information is given on location of map and further references
on author and sources. This relates to Mexican-Americans
as a geographical guide to their Spanish heritage in the U.S.

178   Ludanyi, R. P., and Roselin Ehrlich. Santa Fe Bi-
        lingual-Bicultural Education Programs. New York:
        Hunter College, Bilingual Education Applied Research
        Unit, 1972. 45p. ED 080 023
        Intended to provide a content analysis schedule for the
Bilingual-Bicultural Education program in Santa Fe, New
Mexico. Covers the native and dominant language of students,
information on staff selection, assessment of the bilingual
component, and an analysis of materials, grouping, curriculum, etc. Very good table of contents but no index.
        This is a unique document because it contains the
basic information for setting up a bilingual-bicultural program at the elementary level. It contains objectives, bibliography, and samples of record keeping. The bibliography
has 39 annotated entries on this topic. Highly useful, as it
provides a blueprint.

179   Luna, Juanita J. A Selected Vocabulary of the Spanish
        Spoken in Sabinal, Texas. Master's thesis. San
        Marcos, Texas: Southwest Texas State University,
        1970. 100p.
        The purpose of this study was "to collect, examine,
and record the main features of Spanish vernacular of Sabinal, Texas." The vocabulary was collected from speakers of
all classes in Sabinal. Arranged by introduction, vocabulary,
idiomatic expressions, and conclusions, A Selected Vocabulary
has approximately 490 entries. These are words not found
in standard universal Spanish. The entries are delimited by
11 definers including variants, part of speech, gender, slang,
definition, use in context plus translation and distribution.
Luna has studied the Spanish of one small area and has done
an excellent job of defining the entries. Her study is preceded by a history of the area and has a bibliography with
27 titles. Perhaps the only weakness is lack of detail on
methodology. This work has been subsumed by the Dictionary of the Spanish of Texas by Galvan and Teschner.

180   Lutrell, Estelle. Newspapers and Periodicals of Ari-
        zona, 1859-1911. Tucson: University of Arizona

Press, 1950. 123p.
Records Arizona's territorial newspapers and periodicals; also includes biographical sketches of newspaper men. Arranged alphabetically by city and town with index and chronological list of newspapers.
Each entry has date, language, frequency, editors, and name changes. Although most of the newspapers are English, 18 of the entries refer to the Spanish-language press.

181   McCarthy, Betty Anne.   Legal Services to the Poor; A
      Selective Bibliography. Sacramento: California State
      University Law Library, 1970. 17p.
A listing of all print materials but mainly journal articles from 1954 to 1969, on legal affairs as they relate to the poor. Entries by author under one of the following topics-- legal services and legal aid, public defenders, referral services, and group legal services.
256 unannotated entries. This bibliography is not specifically Mexican American but relates directly to them as a minority both ethnic and economic. Also many of the references refer to California. Aside from an occasional reference to legal services in other bibliographies, this is the only one whose title would definitely encompass the Mexican American.

182   MacCurdy, Raymond R.   A History and Bibliography of
      Spanish Language Newspapers in Louisiana, 1808-1949.
      Albuquerque: University of New Mexico Press, 1951.
      (University of New Mexico Publications in Language
      and Literature, no. 8.) 43p.
Gives brief history of each newspaper: dates, editor, purpose and occasionally a quotation. First 33 pages devoted to history of the 46 papers mentioned in bibliography. Last page devoted to bibliographies of newspapers and works consulted.
The bibliography is the main value since it describes each newspaper plus location of major holdings. Text of work not only describes newspapers but provides a schematic history of the Spanish in Louisiana.

183   MacCurdy, Raymond R.   The Spanish Dialect in St.
      Bernard Parish, Louisiana. Albuquerque: University
      of New Mexico Press, 1950. (University of New Mexico Publications in Language and Literature, no. 6.)

88p.
Basically a dictionary of unique Spanish words from
one region of Louisiana; contains brief studies of the land and
people and the phonology and morphology of the regional Spanish. In addition to the three sections mentioned, there is also an eight-page bibliography of history of Louisiana and
studies of the Spanish language.
Of major value is the dictionary of approximately 700
Spanish words peculiar to the region. Each entry described
by gender, definition and relationship to French and Spanish.
Possibly, the only regional dictionary of Spanish for this
area.

184 McKee, Okla Markham.   Five-Hundred Non-Dictionary
     Words Found in the El Paso-Juarez Press.   Master's
     thesis.   El Paso: Texas Western College, 1955.
     Designed "to present and classify over five-hundred
words found in El Paso-Juarez Spanish publications and not
found in the same form or meaning in six of the dictionaries
in most frequent use in this area. " The body of the work
is on form and meaning with subdivisions on suffixes, ortho-
graphic changes, unlisted meanings, mistranslations, etc.
     This study could serve as a partial dictionary for the
area mentioned.   Although not in alphabetical arrangement,
the words usually are defined and occasionally presented in
context.   Author suggests that this is only a partial study
and that in fact innumerable words do not appear in the
standard dictionaries.

185 McNary, Laura Kelly.   California Spanish and Indian
     Place Names: Their Pronunciation, Meaning, and Lo-
     cation.   Los Angeles: Wetzel Pub. Co. , 1931.   77p.
     A type of gazetteer for non-Anglo place names in
California.   Place names, map of El Camino Real, mountains
and elevations, etc.   The first and most valuable part of
this work is the dictionary of place names each with pronunciation, definition, and location by county.

186 McSpadden, George E.   Some Semantic and Philological
     Facts of the Spanish Spoken in Chilili, New Mexico.
     Written under the direction of F. M. Kercheville.
     Albuquerque: University of New Mexico Press, 1934.
     (University of New Mexico Bulletin Language Series,
     vol. 5.)

Records the unique Spanish of Chilili, N. M. , including history of region, vocabulary, phonology and morphology. Extremely short dictionary compiled by author who spent three months in Chilili. Although author mentions only 90 words, he indicates the area of New Mexico where each is spoken, definition, part of speech, example in a sentence. Brief but informative. In the third section he notes new forms, archaisms, anglicisms, and words of uncertain origin.

187   McVicker, Mary Louise.   The Writings of J. Frank
      Dobie: A Bibliography.   Lawton, Ok. :   Great Plains
      Historical Assoc. , 1968.   258p.
      An attempt at a comprehensive list of all of the works of J. Frank Dobie--books, contributions to the books of others, magazine articles and stories, pamphlets and reprints, and newspapers, arranged in this order, subarranged first chronologically then under author.   Excellent index of author, title, and periodical.
      Looks like a most comprehensive bibliography on Dobie.   Although the Mexican American is not dealt with topically, he is suggested in many of the titles.   Naturally many of the other entries relate to Mexico and to Texas and consequently are peripheral to the Mexican Americans.   This is probably the best beginning on Mexican Americans in the writings of J. Frank Dobie.   Naturally a more topically oriented bibliography would be desirable.

188   Maduell, Charles L. , Jr.   The Romance of Spanish Sur-
      names.   New Orleans, n. p. , 1967.   221p.
      Since eight states border on the Gulf of Mexico, the author thought it wise to determine the origin of many of the Spanish surnames.   This is mainly a dictionary of over 1000 Spanish family names.   However, there are two chapters on history of Spain and the origin and characteristics of Spanish surnames.
      Each name has code indicating frequency of occurrence, geographical origin, and etymology when possible.   Appendixes provide information on Spanish geography and also Basque influence on Spanish surnames.

189   Maida, Peter R. , and John L. McCoy.   The Poor: A
      Selected Bibliography.   Washington, D. C. :   U. S. De-
      partment of Agriculture, Economic Research Service,

1969. 56p.
Presents an interdisciplinary view of poverty so that
the user can see the complex nature of the problem. Covers
approximately 1954 to 1969. Monographs and articles in anthropology, demography, economics, physical and mental
health, psychology, sociology, and social psychology. Entries are alphabetized by author under seven separate headings: general; emergency and identification of poverty;
groups with special problems; the life space: individual and
community; education; resource development problem and
programs; and miscellaneous collection of poverty literature.
Author index and highly detailed table of contents.
        652 unannotated entries. Mexican Americans are
found mainly under minority groups and migrants. Moreover,
much relevant material can be found on the discussion of
poverty as a problem. For in addition to the seven general
headings mentioned above, 19 subtopics are also listed. In
other words, pertinent materials on Chicanos could be found
under elderly, cultural milieu, social class and mobility,
etc. Highly useful.

190 Marambio, John L. Vocabulario español de Temple,
     Texas. Master's thesis. San Marcos, Texas: South-
     west Texas State University, 1970. 109p.
        Marambio in Vocabulario español has collected over
800 words from Temple, Texas, that are not considered
standard Spanish. These words are described by part of
speech, variations, Anglicisms, definition, translation, distribution, etc. Occasionally he presents the word in context.
He precedes his study with a short history of the area. Without as much detail these words have been incorporated into
the Dictionary of the Spanish of Texas by Galvan and Teschner.

191 Marin, Christine N. Bibliography. Tempe: Arizona
     State University, Chicano Studies Project, 1973.
        Guide to all materials related to Mexican Americans
in the Hayden Library at Arizona State University. 665 entries by author and no index.
        This work is deficient for several reasons: no anno-
tations, no limitations established, no non-print materials,
and no creative works by Anglos.

192 Martínez, Al. Rising Voices: Profiles of Hispano-

American Lives.   New York: New American Library,
1974.
   Presents 52 biographical sketches of successful Spanish-speaking Americans, contemporary only. Of these 29
are Mexican Americans. The others are Cuban, Puerto Rican,
and Spanish. Organized alphabetically by surname.
   Intended mainly for younger readers. Laudatory accounts of achievers within the Spanish-speaking community.
Probably main purpose of collection is to inspire pride in la
raza for young people.   The main noticeable omission is of
Mexican-American writers such as the recipients of the
Quinto Sol award.

193   Martínez, Gilbert T.   Bibliography on Mexican-Ameri-
      cans.   Sacramento: Sacramento Unified School Dis-
      trict, 1968.   45p.
   List of monographs on the Mexican American. Since
this bibliography is sponsored by a school district, perhaps
it is meant for the secondary level. Cross section of materials but heavy emphasis on social science and education.
Alphabetized by author. No index and no arrangement by
topic.
      630 unannotated entries. No introduction to orient
user as to purpose and limitations. Probably in 1968 this
was a significant bibliography but now it has been superseded
by the work of Frank Pino (q.v.). Lack of index or topical
arrangement makes this bibliography extremely difficult to
use.

194   Martínez, J. V.   Directory of Spanish Surnamed and
      Native Americans in Science and Engineering.   Roches-
      ter, N.Y., 1972.   33p.
   Intended to aid in establishing communication among
these types of Spanish-surnamed professionals who are concerned about the societal problems of this ethnic group. Limited to scientists and engineers living in the United States.
No suggestion is made as to sources for the list.
      99 alphabetically arranged surnames, including busi-
ness address and phone number; home address and phone
number; birthplace and birthdate; degree, discipline and date
awarded; degree granting institution; and special research interest. An asterisk by the name indicates a commitment to
aid in programs to train Spanish-surnamed and native Americans in science and engineering. Place of birth indicates
that many of those listed are Mexican Americans.

195 Martinez, Julio. Selective Bibliography of Chicano Bib-
     liographies. San Diego, Cal. : San Diego State Uni-
     versity, Malcolm A. Love Library, 1971. 16p.
     Guide to Chicano bibliographies published in the previ-
ous fifteen years. Contains works dealing exclusively with
Mexican Americans or works that devote a large number of
their entries to items on Chicano culture. Arranged alphabetically by author surname.
     Has 151 unannotated entries of Chicano bibliographies.
Generally three types of works--monographs, library holdings,
and bibliographies of article length published in journals.
This work is one of the first that has been published separately on Chicano bibliography. Its orientation is mainly history and social science and it refers the user to another bibliography for works on the humanities. One of its main
values is the listing of bibliographies that are general in
scope and deal with poverty, politics, and bilingual education.

196 Maynes, J. O. ("Rocky"), Jr. (comp.). Books on Mex-
     ican Americans and Recommended Classroom Materi-
     als. Phoenix: Arizona State Dept. of Education, Div.
     of Migrant Education, 1970? 22p.
     A guide to classroom audiovisual materials and mono-
graphs of a Mexican American orientation. Also universal
themes in Spanish. Elementary, junior high and high school.
Arranged by format: visual aids, kits, tapes, films, filmstrips, monographs and microfiche.
     Somewhat dated now, but one of the best bibliographies
with a cross section of print and non-print materials on Mexican Americans. Many of the entries are well annotated.
This is one of the few bibliographies on Mexican Americans
that goes beyond cultural identity, i. e. , it includes films in
Spanish that treat topics of a non-cultural nature. In addition to listing materials, this bibliography also includes distributors of information. Extremely valuable for any teacher
of Mexican American students below the college level.

197 Meier, Matt S. , and Feliciano Rivera. A Bibliography
     for Chicano History. San Francisco: R and E Re-
     search Associates, 1972. 96p.
     Items to help understand each major historical period
of the Mexican American. It is divided into five major historical sections and includes two additional topics, labor and
immigration and civil rights. Section on theses and dissertations. Divides each historical period by books and period-

icals: colonial period, Mexican period, Mexican War to 1900,
1900 to Depression, World War II to the present, labor and
immigration, civil rights, Mexican-American culture, theses
and dissertations, and bibliography. No index and no annotations.

    This bibliography has a very great emphasis on Mexi-
co to show the origins of the Chicano. However, there is
much of value on the Mexican American in the chapter on
labor and civil rights and the final section on bibliography.
Missing is a listing of the major indexes and abstracts that
might aid the user to know contemporary developments. A
subject index would have facilitated use. No mention of non-
print materials.

198   Metzler, William and Frederic O. Sargent. Migratory
      Farmworkers in the Midcontinent Stream. Washing-
      ton, D.C.: U.S. Dept. of Agriculture in Cooperation
      with Texas Agricultural Experiment Station, 1960.
      62p.

    Provides more precise knowledge on the types of la-
borers in the migratory labor force, mainly south Texas
from 1956-57. Details characteristics of South Texan migrants, their annual migration patterns, recruitment and
movement, employment and unemployment, earnings, rates of
pay, social security, etc., arranged in this order. No index
but list of sources.

    A study now dated but with information that is prob-
ably still pertinent. 34 tables of statistics. South Texas incorporates six home-base cities: San Antonio, Crystal City,
Eagle Pass, Laredo, Weslaco, and Robstown. Very accessible information on ages, place of birth, education, age when
began migratory farm work, month of departures, media for
information concerning jobs, etc. Also has graphs of major
migratory routes within Texas and interstate. Much explanatory text makes this a highly useful source of information on
migrant labor in Texas.

199   Mexican American (Chicano) Handbook of Affirmative
      Action Programs for Employers and Employees and a
      Directory of Governmental-Industrial-Educational-Com-
      munity Agencies and Representatives. Downey, Cal.:
      Personnel Management Assoc. of Aztlán, 1973. 170p.
      ED 082 866.

    Designed "to promote the full utilization of Chicano
talents and skills in every area and stratum of society." Has

six chapters: what affirmative action means, government
compliance agencies, high schools and colleges available,
man power and training sources are essential, Chicano government representatives, and national Chicano organizations.
    This is an invaluable work to aid the Chicano in an
area where he has often suffered discrimination, i. e. , employment. It provides charts, samples of forms, text of
laws, etc. to aid him to find employment. It also has a
directory of Chicano Affirmative Action representatives to
serve as a source for information for students and other
members of the Chicano community.

200 Mexican-American Legal Defense and Educational Fund.
     A Progress Report, n. p. , n. d.   20p.
    The history, function, and scope of MALDEF: brief
history, operations, organizational charts, program accom-
plishments, regional offices and referral attorney program,
educational grants, special projects, program support, and
financial report, arranged in this order.
    This is an important reference work for Mexican
Americans who want information on organization in defense
of La Raza. The text and charts are clear and understandable. Apparently MALDEF's goal is the promotion of civil
rights through legal action and education. Lists regional
offices and board of directors and their location.

201 Mexican American Task Force of the Synod of Texas.
     The Mexican American Churches in the Synod of Texas.
     Kingsville, Texas: Presbyterian Pan American School,
     1971. 22p.
    Current data on the churches and clergy of the Mexi-
can American churches in the Synod of Texas of the Presbyterian Church in the United States. Covers 1960 to 1969,
name of church, date established, pastoral care, membership
gains and losses, biographical information on pastors, etc.
    A brief but succinct directory that serves as an index
to this church's activities among Mexican Americans in Texas.
One of the few such directories that exists among Protestant
churches.

202 Mexican Americans in Texas History.   Big Spring,
     Texas: Creative Visuals, 1971.
    Presents in a visual form the biographical sketches of
famous, mainly 19th-century Texans of Mexican descent.

These are 12 individual transparencies arranged alphabetically.
This is a novel way to present biographical sketches
to students from the elementary grades through high school.
They are to be used on an overhead projector and each of
the 12 transparencies has a picture of the subject and a laudatory summary of his life in approximately 50 words. Hopefully the series will continue and incorporate Chicanos from
the 20th century.   Excellent for cultural identification especially for younger Chicanos.   This kit includes: Francita
"Panchita" Alvez, Santos Benavides, Jesús Cuéllar "Co-
manche," José María Carbajal, José de Escandón, Manual
Joaquín Gonzales, José Antonio Navarro, Juan N. Seguín,
Juan Martín Veramendi, Antonio Zapata, Ignacio Zaragoza,
and Lorenzo de Zavala.

203 Mexican-Fact Finding Committee. Mexicans in Cali-
      fornia.   San Francisco: R and E Research Associates,
      1970. 214p.
      Presents "facts relating to the industrial, social and
agricultural aspects of the problems of Mexican immigration
into California."   Covers 1920's to 1928.   Immigration, popular and naturalization; Mexicans in industries and in nonagri-
cultural occupations; labor needs in California crop production; health, relief and delinquency; and the Mexican family,
its size and income, arranged in this order with each of
these sections further refined.   Detailed table of contents
and list of tables.   No index.
      This is a 1970 reprint of a 1928 brief but informative
study, supported by 100 charts and tables.   Must be one of
the most complete reports of the Mexican in California in
the 1920's.   No explanation available on how statistics were
gathered.   In spite of this defect the work is invaluable.

204 Michigan Education Association. A Selected Bibliogra-
      phy of Material Relating to Racism, Blacks, Chicanos,
      Native Americans, and Multi Ethnicity.   East Lansing:
      Michigan Education Association, 1971. 75p. ED 069
      445
      Presents material that the Michigan Education Asso-
ciation "believes to be most representative of the realities
that relate to the involvement and contributions of ... Chicanos..."   Provides educators with a practical instrument
to foster awareness of multi ethnicity.   In relation to the
Mexican American this provides a guide to monographs and

films, mainly of a historical or social science orientation. Approximately 64 descriptively annotated citations of this nature.

Although the compilers limited their entries mainly to works on the Mexican American, or related studies in the section on racism materials, they omitted an extremely important body of Chicano literature by both Anglos and Mexican Americans--creative literature, i. e., poetry, short stories and novels. Only six films and filmstrips included.

205 Michigan State University. Libraries. Finding Chicano
Materials in the Michigan State University Libraries.
East Lansing: Michigan State University Libraries,
1973. (How to Find Series, no. 1.) 16p.

Intended to familiarize the inexpert user not only with Mexican-American materials but also with the most appropriate search strategy to locate such materials. Lists Mexican American and some Puerto Rican materials in all formats. Arranged alphabetically by format and genre.

Most guides to small collection are not worth evaluating. This one is an exception in that it attempts to orient the user to terminology, subject headings, and the peculiar tools necessary to using each format. Actually has few entries but is invaluable as a guide to further materials on Mexican Americans.

206 Mignon, Molly. Chicanos: A Bibliography of Government Documents and Pamphlets on the Mexican American [mimeo.]. Bellingham: Western Washington State
College, 1970. 4p.

This is a list of the uncatalogued materials in the Wilson Library of the above institution. It contains government documents and pamphlets that relate to the Mexican American. All of the materials run from approximately 1962 to 1969. Mignon divides this short bibliography into two sections: government documents, and pamphlets. In the first part materials are arranged according to the government body that produced them--i. e., U. S. Commission on Civil Rights, HEW, etc. The pamphlets are arranged alphabetically by author. A total of 37 entries are included in this bibliography.

Although the government documents have descriptive annotations, the pamphlets have only basic bibliographical information. This bibliography is now dated and for actual use in research its value may be limited. However, it is an excellent example of what a library can do to make the patron

aware of government documents and ephemera on Mexican
Americans. This type of material is often overlooked by the
unsophisticated library user.

207 Mickey, Barbara H. A Bibliography of Studies Concern-
     ing the Spanish-Speaking Population of the American
     Southwest. Greeley: Colorado State College, 1969.
     (Museum of Anthropology Miscellaneous Series, no. 4.)
     42p.
     "Gather[s] together references useful to an anthropo-
logical study of the Spanish-speaking population of the American Southwest. " Books, articles and dissertations from the
1930's to mid 1960's, arranged alphabetically by author.
Books and articles integrated.
     544 unannotated entries. "Anthropological" here in-
corporates ethnography, sociology, and education. A topical
index would have facilitated use.

208 Migrant Education: A Selected Bibliography (with ERIC
     abstracts). Washington, D. C. : GPO, 1973. (ERIC/
     CRESS suppl. no. 3.) 159p.
     Designed "to provide access to some of the latest re-
search findings and developments on migrant education. "
Materials from Research in Education and Current Index to
Journals in Education. RIE articles from April 1970 to Sep-
tember 1972 and CIJE articles from December 1970 to Sep-
tember 1972. Arranged in three sections--citations from
RIE, CIJE citations, and index to both.
     Another excellent ERIC/CRESS bibliography and ab-
stract with almost 300 entries. Each with accession number,
publication date, title, author, descriptor, identifiers, price,
and description, which is sufficiently long to indicate if article is pertinent--or is perhaps even a substitution for reading. This bibliography is a supplement to three previous
ERIC/CRESS publications. Index has 25 entries on Mexican
Americans and numerous topics that could relate to this ethnic group.

209 Miller, Levi (ed.). Mennonite Yearbook and Directory,
     1974, vol. 65. Scottdale, Pa. : Mennonite Pub.
     House, 1974. 144p.
     Directory to Mennonite congregations in the U. S. and
the rest of the world. In a compact form, gives listing of
ministers and the activities of churches for U. S. and world.

Has table of contents with 13 subdivisions and also a three-
page index.

Main value of this directory is that out of the 2747
ministers listed, 37 are ministers to Spanish-speaking congregations, although it is difficult to find these 37 in the
book except for an occasional reference to a Spanish name.
However, directory also has two-page supplement listing ministers for Spanish-speaking congregations.

210 Miller, Margaret (comp.). Las Comidas; Recipes in
     English and Spanish from the Kitchens of Texas
     Homes. n. p. , n. d.
     Collection of Mexican recipes from central Texas.
Recipes gathered from Austin, Ennis, Georgetown, Lampasas,
San Marcos, San Saba, and Seguin. Basic entries such as
breads, sauces, etc. No index or table of contents. Book
is divided into sauces, breads, vegetables, desserts, and
meats.

     Approximately 100 recipes. This cookbook may be
considered superior to the others for one reason--the recipes
are in both Spanish and English. According to the preface
this is the first time that many of these recipes have been
recorded.

211 Mindiola, Tatcho. A Demographic Profile of Texas and
     Selected Cities; Some Recent Trends, 1950-1970.
     Houston, Texas: Houston University, Center for Hu-
     man Resources, 1974. 59p. ED 097 147.
     An analysis of population changes within Texas from
1950 to 1970 from the point of view of growth, components
of growth, and distribution. This study is based on 12 statistical references on Texas. In addition to the United States
census reports, Mindiola also has used the Browning & Mc-
Lemore work (q. v.).

     Much of this study relates to the Mexican American
who in the 20 years has: increased numerically; remained
proportionately the same in relation to Blacks and Anglos;
been migratory within Texas; and gravitated to metropolitan
areas. The study seems well researched and is supported
by 23 tables and four maps. Although not tendentious, Mindiola thinks that Blacks and Chicanos have been undernumer-
ated. Abstracts much statistical information on the Chicano
for a 20-year period.

212 Moreno, H. M. Moreno's Dictionary of Spanish-Named
     California Cities and Towns. San Luis Obispo, Cal.,
     n. p., 1916. 95p.
     Presents correct pronunciation and definition of Spanish
cities, towns and counties in California.
     Approximately 240 names of cities and towns in dic-
tionary arrangement. Only gives pronunciation and definition.
The longer section on names of counties is composed of a
short paragraph on each county. This section also includes
non-Spanish names.

213 Moreno, Raul. Directory of Minority Racial/Ethnic
     Members in the Church of the Brethren [mimeographed].
     La Verne, Cal., 1973. 9p.
     Guide to minority groups within this church group:
American Indians, Blacks, Asians, and Latin Americans, arranged in this order but "Latin American" refers to Mexican
Americans, Puerto Ricans and Cubans.
     Brief but hopefully other Protestant groups will pro-
vide similar directories. Each entry with name of member,
address, and occupation; 33 Mexican Americans mentioned.

214 Moyer, June, Lydia Chavez, and Anthony Trujillo.
     Chicano Bibliography of Bi-cultural Material in the
     SCSC Library. Alamosa: Southern Colorado State
     College Library, 1971. 19p.
     A guide to the Chicano materials at the college--mon-
ographs, government documents, and the vertical file. Selection from all disciplines on Mexico and Mexican Americans.
Arranged alphabetically under disciplines. In addition to
disciplines, has other categories such as government documents, reference books, and periodical indexes.
     Rather a traditional holdings list of a college library
collection. Like many, this one establishes no guidelines for
inclusions. Its main contribution is the entry on vertical file
materials. This bibliography has a recent six-page supplement on la Chicana.

215 Muniz, Ramsey. Ramsey Muniz '74 Campaign. Corpus
     Christi, Texas: Mirabel Printing Co. [1974]? 16p.
     Suggestions on how to run a successful political cam-
paign. Covers campaign strategy, organizing the local campaign, fund raising, developing materials, getting the most
for the least, etc. Arranged in the above order.

This is a highly practical and pragmatic manual that tells how to conduct a successful political campaign. It is a guide for the amateur who must raise his own funds and support. Relates to Mexican Americans as the suggestions apparently are based on the experiences of the Ramsey Muniz campaign.

216 National Migrant Information Clearing House. Migrant Programs in the Southwestern States: Arizona, Colorado, Kansas, Nevada, New Mexico, and Utah. Austin, Texas: Juarez-Lincoln Center, 1974. 173p.

Designed "to consolidate under one cover a listing of all services and resources available to migrant and seasonal farmworkers during their stay in the states here included." The five states are analyzed by programs for migrant and seasonal workers, crops and work periods, migrant population and wages by county, labor camps, and supplementary information. Arranged by state, and subarranged by the above topics.

Invaluable information either to the migrant or to those who wish to assist the migrant. For example, lists schools and addresses that participate in the Migrant Child Education program, information on the obtaining of the GED diploma, health projects, legal aid, agencies which may assist migrants and labor camps. Also available with a varying format but similar information are publications on the other states that have migrant workers. These were compiled by the Juarez Lincoln Center of the National Migrant Information Clearing House in Austin, Texas.

217 National Union Catalog of Manuscript Collections, 1959/ 1972. Hamden, Conn.: Shoe String, n.d. 10 vols.

Indicates manuscript holdings in 400 depositories of the United States. Includes cards for over 12,000 manuscript collections. All topics, including Mexican Americans. Each entry provides number of items, physical description, contents, location, availability, etc. Collection also notes personal papers such as letters, diaries, memoranda, etc. Biennial cumulative indexes. Integrated index of author and subject leads to numbered paragraphs--extremely easy to use.

Unfortunately in the ten volumes of manuscripts there are only nine entries on Mexican Americans. Yet these could be fruitful to the serious investigator, e.g., Tucson and its Mexican population, the Sleepy Lagoon Case, migrant labor in California, Texas Presbyterians of Mexican descent,

folklore, Juan Cortina, temperance work among Mexican
Americans, and the labor archives at Wayne State University.
Mexican Americans are doubtlessly incorporated under some
other headings. This reference work indicates the need for
the finding and maintenance of Chicano archives.

218   Navarro, E. G.   Annotated Bibliography of Materials on
      the Mexican Americans.   Austin: University of Texas,
      1969.   53p.
      Locates and annotates available literature and films in
the various fields of social science and related disciplines.
Not divided by discipline.   No table of contents or index.
      Access is difficult because of lack of index.   131 en-
tries, books and other publications, with extended annotations
that summarize and evaluate book.   Limited to social science,
i. e. , nothing on literature.   Nothing on Mexico.

219   Navarro, Eliseo.   The Chicano Community: A Selected
      Bibliography for Use in Social Work Education.   New
      York: Council on Social Work Education, 1971.   57p.
      Provides the material necessary for social workers to
understand the quality of life of the Mexican American.
Mainly articles and books from social science, history and
literature of the 1960's, divided by format, i. e. , books and
articles.   No index or table of contents.
      Approximately 150 annotated entries.   Each has com-
plete bibliographic entry plus a code letter that indicates the
subject for which the described material would be useful:
historical and background data; acculturation and culture con-
flict; issues and problems; power, politics and the Chicano
community; Chicano organizations; economics and the Chicano
community; social welfare and social work; the Chicano family; literature; and reference material.   Excellent annotations
of 100 words or more that summarize and at the same time
criticize the works.

220   Newman, Patty.   ¡Do It up Brown!   San Diego, Cal. :
      Viewpoint Books, 1971.   392p.
      A guide to radical chicanismo--mainly, the recency of
the Chicano movement as shown through its leaders and its
militant organizations.   Divided into four main sections--
definitions, biographies, Chicano organizations, and activism
of the Chicanos.   No index.
      One of the few explanations of militant chicanismo

through its leaders and organizations. The author is completely subjective and praises or criticizes when she sees fit.
Has three biographies and gives origin and goals of 14 Chicano organizations.

221 New Mexico. Employment Security Commission. Mi-
     nority Groups in New Mexico. Santa Fe, n. p. , n. d.
     73p.
     Focuses on employment problems and minority groups
in New Mexico. Spanish surname, Negro and Indian are the
minority groups under consideration. Chapters on Employment Security Commission in New Mexico; general population
characteristics of New Mexico; employment and income; employment income, and education; civil rights legislation, etc. ,
arranged in that order. Guide to tables and maps.
     Although the purpose of this is the employment of
minority groups, this study provides much valuable information regarding the Hispanos of New Mexico. The information
is easily apprehended in the tables and maps: composition
of population, Hispano population by counties, percent of
ethnic group to total population, unemployment rates, persons
with and without income, educational level, etc. The problem is that the statistics are based on the 1960 census.

222 New Mexico. Historical Records Survey. Guide to
     Public Vital Statistics Records in New Mexico. Albu-
     querque, 1942. 135p.
     A guide to the vital statistics records and a discussion
of the laws for the maintenance of such statistics. Births,
deaths, marriages, divorces, and church records (from ca.
1697 to ca. 1941), arranged in this order. Also has index
of births, deaths, and marriages by counties and a subject
index.
     Although ethnic groups not specified here, much of
the material relates to the Hispanos. Birth records are
listed under alphabetized counties and described by year and
type of name entry. Death and marriage listed in a similar
manner but in separate sections. Of special interest to the
Mexican American is the listing of baptisms, marriages and
deaths in the Spanish missions. Probably highly useful for
genealogy. This is a primary source for vital statistics in
New Mexico. Similar guides with varying formats are also
available for Arizona, California, Colorado and Texas.

223   New Mexico (Territory).   Secretary's Office.   New Mex-
      ico Blue Book, 1882.   Compiled by W. G. Ritch,
      Secretary of the Territory.   Albuquerque: University
      of New Mexico Press, 1968.   154p.
         Manual on New Mexican territorial government de-
signed for legislators.   Presents the structure of the government in 1882 and is filled with miscellaneous records such
as public land system, railway distances, etc.   Has table of
contents and an excellent topical index.
         Mainly a chronicle of the New Mexico Territory of
1882, this work also has specific reference value concerning
Mexican Americans--a section on private land claims, a
chronology of the territory's history, county population, i.e.,
native, foreign, and white, and the legislative assembly from
1847 to 1881.   This includes many Hispano names.   In short
a valuable, interesting guide.

224   Newton, Charles H.   The Reason Why Place Names in
      Arizona Are So Named.   Phoenix, Ariz.:   Charles H.
      Newton Pub. Co., 1954.   47p.
         Guide to origin of over 700 Arizona place names.
Covers counties and communities in a dictionary arrangement.
         Counties with date of origin; communities with counties
in which they are located.   Both with a definition of the name.
Many of the entries indicate a Spanish origin.

225   New York City.   Board of Education.   Bilingual ERIC
      Publications.   Brooklyn: Bilingual Resource Center,
      1973.   12p.   ED 081 280
         A listing of ERIC processed documents on bilingual
education.   Divided into four sections: introduction, documents of general interest, English as a second language, and
Spanish speakers.   Approximately 100 unannotated entries of
both monographs and articles on microfiche.
         As the section labels indicate, this bibliography is in-
tended mainly for English/Spanish bilingual education.   The
work would date quickly because the compilers predict that
the Center will be adding approximately 20 titles per month
on this subject.   Very good for the educator who has access
to ERIC microfiche.

226   Nichols, Margaret S., and Margaret N. O'Neill.   Multi-
      cultural Bibliography for Preschool Through Second
      Grade: In the Areas of Black, Spanish-speaking, Asian

Americans, and Native American Cultures. Stanford, Cal. : Multicultural Resources, 1972. 40p.

Bibliography of works on Blacks, Mexican Americans, and Asian Americans for pre-third graders. Includes books for children, materials for parents and teachers, directory of publishers, other written materials, posters, songs, etc. Arranged by ethnic group and then by special sections for teachers and parents, professional materials and multi-ethnic bibliographies. Index of titles and table of contents.

Approximately 750 unannotated entries. Well organized except there is no topical index. Over 100 titles listed for the Spanish-speaking. Also three pages of entries on multi-cultural materials. The section on materials for parents and teachers is especially unique. Also the 45 entries on multi-ethnic bibliographies is not found in most works of this nature. One of the best bibliographies for materials for pre-third graders.

227 Nichols, Margaret S. , and Margaret N. O'Neill. Multicultural Materials: A Selective Bibliography of Adult Materials Concerning Human Relations and the History, Culture and Current Social Issues of Black, Chicano, Asian American and Native American Peoples. Stanford, Cal. : Multicultural Resources, 1974. 49p.

A guide to basic collection items (monographs and major periodicals--not articles) on Blacks, Chicanos, Asian Americans, and Native Americans. Alphabetical entries under separate cultures. No index.

Approximately 150 entries under Chicanos. Good cross-section of materials for core collections for public libraries and high schools. Major fault is no criteria given as to reasons for inclusions. The directory of publishers would have been more useful if it had indicated the ethnic specialization of each publisher.

228 Oakland [Cal.] Public Library. A Basic Collection for Spanish Speaking Patrons. Oakland, Cal. : Latin American Library, 1969? 38p.

A guide to books, newspapers and magazines, and audiovisual materials that Spanish-speaking patrons might like. Mexican and Mexican American themes and any other works that might interest this clientele. Mainly those published since 1950. Author entry under one of the three formats covered. No index or table of contents.

Approximately 240 annotated entries. The entries on

the Mexican Americans and Mexico are rather standard.
However, this is one of the few bibliographies that lists
works that a Mexican American might want to read, i.e.,
a Mexican American who has no interest in la raza but
wants general information.   This bibliography provides an
excellent list for any public library, i.e., how-to-do it books
and popular American novels in translation.   Indispensable
for any library with Spanish-speaking clientele or any library
school training librarians for minority groups.

229   Oakland [Cal.] Public Schools.   The Mexican Americans:
      Books for Young People.   Oakland, Cal.:   Oakland
      Public Schools, Div. of Instructional Media, 1969.
      27p.
         An attempt to cite suitable materials on Mexican Amer-
icans for Oakland school children.   Divided into two sections:
Mexicans in the United States, and those in Mexico.   No index.
         This is an early effort to create a bibliography on
Mexican Americans.   Consequently, one can overlook the
lack of guidelines as to what is pertinent for reading materials for this ethnic group.   The major part of this bibliography unfortunately concerns works on Mexico.   Approximately
200 titles listed with basic bibliographical information and a
brief descriptive annotation.   Coding indicates suitability of
materials for high school or junior high school.   Copy examined was obtained from Oakland Public Schools.

230   O'Dwyer, Carlota Cárdenas de.   Chicano Literature:
      An Introduction and an Annotated Bibliography [mimeo-
      graphed].   Austin: University of Texas, Department
      of English and Mexican-American Studies, 1973.   22p.
         Main purpose is to identify the word Chicano and note
the creative literature done mainly by Chicanos.   Contains
43 entries (16 annotated) on all aspects and genres of Chicano literature, i.e., novel, drama, poetry, anthologies,
bibliography, and criticism.   Arranged alphabetically by
genre.   Brevity precludes need for index.
         Interesting introduction on the language and purpose
of Chicano literature.   One of the few bibliographies that
makes prescriptive annotations of the creative works of la
raza.   Although not stated, the apparent purpose is to limit
the bibliography to works written by Chicanos.   This excludes
the innumerable titles mentioned in Cecil Robinson's With the
Ears of Strangers; The Mexican in American Literature.

231   Onouye, Wendy.   A Guide to Materials for Ethnic Stud-
      ies, rev. ed.   Seattle: Shoreline Community College,
      Learning Resources Center, 1972.   178p.   ED 090 111
      Guide to ethnic studies materials in the Learning Re-
sources Center of Shoreline Community College.   Covers
materials published in the 1960's and 1970's on non-white
ethnic groups and race relations, Afro-American, Asia-
American, Mexican American, and Native American, arranged
in that order.   Listing by type of material: reference books
and microforms, periodicals and newspapers, and media materials.   No index.
      Approximately 465 unannotated citations on Mexican
Americans.   Subject headings for this group are alien labor,
agricultural laborers, Chicanos, Mexican Americans, Mexicans in the U.S., migrant labor and Spanish Americans.
Has far too many entries on Mexico.   Completely ignores
creative fiction on Chicanos.   Too heavily oriented to the
social sciences.

232   Ortego, Philip D.   Selective Mexican American Bibli-
      ography.   El Paso, Texas: Border Regional Library
      Association in cooperation with the Chicano Research
      Institute.   1972.   121p.
      Designed "to bring together information about those
works by Mexican Americans in a number of fields and categories."   Divided into 16 arbitrarily selected categories--
yet many of these appear to mix unrelated disciplines, e.g.,
philosophy and media.   No index.
      Approximately 1610 unannotated entries.   Excluding
corporate entries, only authors of Spanish surname included.
Inclusion criteria not well defined for works from Mexico.

233   Oxnam, G. Bromley.   The Mexican in Los Angeles:
      Los Angeles City Survey.   San Francisco: R and E
      Research Associates Reprint, 1970.   28p.
      A brief view of the Mexicans in Los Angeles in 1920:
housing, illiteracy, health conditions, crime, occupation,
poverty, Protestant work among Mexicans, immigration,
emigration, etc., arranged in this order.   Book is extremely short, so approximately one to two pages for each of the
topics.
      Rather a primitive survey sponsored by the Inter-
church World Movement of North America.   No statement as
to procedure of statistics collecting.   Probably the main value
lies in a summary of Protestant work among Mexican Ameri-

94   Reference Materials

cans. Gives location of church, budget, and activities a-
mong Mexicans.

234 Padgett, James Foyil (comp.). A Documented History
     of the Flores Family, 1725-1963, and Related Fami-
     lies. Ennis, Texas, n.p. , 1963. 257p.
     A genealogical guide to the Flores family, one of the
first from Spain to come to Texas. Runs from 1725 to 1957.
Covers family mainly in Nacogdoches, Texas, and Natchi-
toches, Louisiana. Divided into 11 chapters: history of
Texas, Gil Flores family, José Flores family, Vital Flores
family, José Policarpio Flores family, William Flores family, Katherine Belle Flores Padgett family, other census records, newspapers notices and other records. No index. Author provides a brief descriptive history of the Nacogdoches
area. Also gives genealogy of the Flores family that apparently coincides with the history of Nacogdoches. In addition
the compiler provides genealogical data on many more Spanish-surname families whose names appear with the Flores.
     The compiler has utilized at least nine separate genea-
logical archives in Texas and a smaller number in Louisiana.
Useful for genealogical records of la raza and as a guideline
as to availability of genealogical records and sources. This
copy in the rare books room of the library of Stephen F.
Austin State University in Nacogdoches, Texas.

235 Padilla, Amado M. , and Paul Aranda. Latino Mental
     Health: Bibliography and Abstracts. National Insti-
     tute of Mental Health. Santa Barbara: University of
     California, 1974.
     Guide to psychological and mental health literature by
and about Latinos in the United States. Includes Spanish-
surname, Spanish-speaking and Spanish origin individuals.
Material taken from Psychological Abstracts through 1972.
Covers all areas of psychological and mental health. Arranged alphabetically by author. Has subject index.
     497 articles reviewed. Each with complete biblio-
graphical entry from anthropological, psychological, and sociological journals. Excellent abstracts (190 words) that
carefully delineate the articles' themes and are almost a
substitute for reading. "Latinos" here refers mainly to
Puerto Ricans and Mexican Americans.

236 Padilla, Ray. Apuntes para la documentación de la cul-

tura chicana. El Grito, vol. V, no. 2 (winter 1971-72). Berkeley, Cal.: Quinto Sol Publications, 1972. 79p.

A bibliography of bibliographies of materials relating to the Chicanos. Padilla also evaluates Chicano bibliography from 1846 to 1972. Lists 513 bibliographies of print materials on the Mexican American. Includes almost all subjects within Chicanismo. A 43-page bibliographical essay precedes the 513 entries alphabetized by author surname. No indexing. The compiler, Ray Padilla, has contributed 55 entries. The remaining 453 are those of Joseph A. Clark Moreno. Each entry has basic bibliographical material and no annotations.

The lack of subject divisions and an index makes use of this work difficult. However, value is in the multiple topics included that relate directly and also peripherally to the Chicano. Of interest is Padilla's tendentious bibliographical essay in which he provides a state of the art assessment on Chicano bibliography. He advocates a Chicano point of view and deplores much of the work done by Anglos, "gabachos." Although he has surveyed the field, he too is confused on what to do with Mexico for several of his entries concerning this country do not seem even peripheral to the Chicano. This work is valuable for those who would attempt to do a Chicano bibliography. However, it is a frustration for the user who is searching for a particular topic.

237 Page, Mrs. Clarence, and Mrs. T. J. Williamson. The Role of Minority Groups in Texas History. Kilgore, Texas: Region VII Education Service Center, 1971. 17p.

A guide to minority groups in Texas for seventh graders. Blacks, Germans, Jews, and Mexican Americans in monographs, articles and audiotapes.

Although too diluted because of its scope, this is the only bibliography that is specifically for seventh-grade teachers. Nine entries with descriptive annotations. Also 11 entries that apply to more than one minority group. This work should be expanded and improved, for too few bibliographies cite materials meant for junior high schools.

238 Palacios Arturo (ed.). The Mexican-American Directory. Washington, D. C.: Executive Systems Corps, 1969. 210p.

Provides a list to identify professionals and paraprofessionals of Mexican American origin, nationwide, who have

achieved visibility regardless of academic credentials. A
few people from other ethnic groups who have contributed to
the Mexican American community have also been included in
this book.

Approximately 828 entries alphabetized by surname,
with date of birth, education, name of spouse, military background, memberships, profession and activities, and home address.

239   Pan American Union.   Division of Labor and Social In-
      formation.   Mexicans in the United States: A Bibli-
      ography.   Washington: Pan American Union, 1942.
      (Bibliographic Series, 27.)   14p.
      Supplements the bibliography of Emory S. Bogardus
(q. v.) of 1929.   All but one entry on books and articles
written in English since 1929.   Covers social science with
emphasis on emigration.   Arranged thus: general, urban
settlements and industrial labor, agricultural labor, fiction
(five entries), and social problems of Mexicans in the United
States.   No index.
      Approximately 224 unannotated items, mainly journal
articles.

240   Pascual, Henry, et al.   Diccionario Bilingue-Cultural;
      Bilingual Cultural Dictionary.   Santa Fe, N. M. :
      Santa Fe Public School, 1974.   50p.
      This dictionary is considered a necessary component
of the first year bilingual/bicultural program of New Mexico.
Contains simple words and concepts in Spanish and English
but with a definite orientation to New Mexico.   Alphabetically
arranged by Spanish word entry.
      Approximately 100 words in Spanish with definitions
and beautiful accompanying illustrations.   On the opposite of
each page of entries in Spanish are their equivalents in English.   This dictionary shows much imagination in meeting
the needs in the lower grades for materials.   Especially at-
tractive is the regional orientation.

241   Patton, Stella Herrera.   Recruitment Resource Manual.
      Austin, Texas: Office of the Governor, 1975.   69p.
      "This manual has been prepared for Texas State Gov-
ernment by the Governor's Office of Equal Employment Opportunity ... to assist state agencies in implementing more
comprehensive Affirmative Acion Programs by providing a

means of reaching, locating and recruiting minority and female applicants for state employment. " Includes recruitment processes, media, minority civic and service organizations, women's organizations, and educational institutions.
Although the Chicanos share this reference work with
Blacks and females, they do predominate. The first part
provides step-by-step instructions on the best methods for
recruiting minorities. The major portion of the manual,
however, lists sources for finding minority candidates. Under each division, cities are listed alphabetically and under
these are addresses of pertinent media, organizations, and
educational institutions. Valuable for anyone who wishes to
locate organizations or personnel with Chicano interests.

242   Pearce, Thomas Matthew (ed.). New Mexico Place
      Names: A Geographical Dictionary.   Albuquerque:
      University of New Mexico Press, 1965. 187p.
      A guide to 5000 alphabetically arranged place names
in New Mexico including all counties and county seats, all
post offices and those discontinued before 1964, parks, monu-
ments, cities, settlements, land grants, lakes, mountains,
etc.
      Innumerable Spanish names included, e. g. , San and Santo
appear 152 times. Each entry has county designation, language from which it is derived, and some history for the
more important Spanish entries. The capital, Santa Fe, has
approximately half a page.

243   Peterson, Clarence Stewart. Consolidated Bibliography
      of County Histories in Fifty States in 1961. Balti-
      more: Genealogical Pub. Co. , 1963. 186p.
      This work attempts to list all county histories of 100
pages or more. It is arranged alphabetically by state and
each entry has the following information: title, author, publisher, date and place of publication, number and size of
pages, price, edition, and descriptive information such as
photos, maps, etc.
      Naturally the five major states of Chicano concentra-
tion, Arizona, California, Colorado, New Mexico, and Texas,
are mentioned. A total of 421 county histories for the Southwest are included. These books may contain much invaluable
genealogical information: biographical sketches, patterns of
settlement, religion, social conditions, etc. Although mainly
Anglo, this can be considered a Mexican American reference
book for its sources on the Southwest.

244   Pino, Frank. Mexican Americans; A Research Bibli-
      ography. East Lansing: Michigan State University,
      Latin American Studies Center, 1974. 2 vols., 1359p.
      An interdisciplinary guide to the study of the Mexican
American. This is an attempt to be the most comprehensive
guide to materials on the Mexican American to date, and is
probably the most universal in coverage. Includes the traditional categories such as economics, anthropology, sociology,
etc. Yet also has sections on the separate southwestern
states, United States History, Spain in America, and cinema
and television. All formats except newspaper articles. The
two volumes are divided into 35 general areas. Entry is provided by table of contents listing the subject areas, and an
author index, both personal and corporate. Some cross references.
      Approximately 8692 unannotated entries. According
to the introduction Pino has availed himself of all the major
sources on Mexican Americans. Although some of the entries are peripheral to the Mexican American experience,
they will provide background sources for the scholar who
can now see what is available in the field. One of the few
bibliographies that lists creative materials on Mexican Americans by Anglos. Better indexing would have facilitated use,
i.e., a page reference in author index rather than a subject
abbreviation. Yet completeness is monumental.

245   Pinto, Patrick R., and Jeanne O. Buchmeier. Prob-
      lems and Issues in the Employment of Minority, Dis-
      advantaged and Female Groups: An Annotated Bibli-
      ography. Minneapolis: University of Minnesota, 1973.
      (Industrial Relations Center, Bulletin no. 59.) 62p.
      Covers monographs, abstracts, and articles from July
2, 1965, through summer of 1972. General reference sources,
legal context, topics in reference to general disadvantaged
groups, and topics in reference to specific groups, i.e.,
Blacks, other racial minorities, etc.
      20 annotated references to Chicanos, Puerto Ricans,
and Cubans. Approximately 224 annotated entries that apply
in general to minorities, disadvantaged, and female groups.
This is the only bibliography in this study that relates to the
legal issues and problems in hiring practices of Chicanos.
Although the Mexican American is generally subsumed in the
three groups mentioned in the title, this bibliography provides
a resourceful context for studying the multiple aspects of
Chicano employment.

246 Pollock, Saul. Dictionary of Spanish and Mexican Given Names. Los Angeles: Committee for Social Research, 1940. 75p.
Provides a reference of Spanish and Mexican given names for those who deal with Spanish-speaking people. Approximately 2200 popular Spanish surnames, alphabetically arranged. Each entry is classified under three separate columns--gender; class, i.e., Biblical, diminutive, etc.; derivation, i.e., the saint's name or other source from which the name originated; and the English equivalent.
Extremely handy. Indispensable especially for the Anglo who works with Mexican Americans.

247 Potter, Helen Rose. Social and Economic Dimensions of Health and Illness Behavior in New Mexico; An Annotated Bibliography. Albuquerque: University of New Mexico Press, 1969. 220p.
Designed "to facilitate access to social and economic information pertinent to health and illness behavior." Covers monographs and articles, 1950 to 1967, for all ethnic groups in New Mexico. Entries taken mainly from New Mexico libraries but also UCLA bookstore, and the Government Printing Office. Divided into two sections--the annotated bibliography, and the four indexes. Entries can be located under ethnic groups, selected categories, and geographical areas.
Approximately 850 descriptively annotated entries easy to locate because of excellent indexing. Almost 350 of these entries relate to Mexican Americans. From subjects listed under Spanish American, it appears that almost every topic has been included. This is one of the best bibliographies on New Mexico and is almost a holding list on Mexican Americans in the State of New Mexico.

248 Potts, Alfred M. Knowing and Educating the Disadvantaged; An Annotated Bibliography. Alamosa, Col.: Center for Cultural Studies, Adams State College, 1965. 460p.
Compilation of entries relating to the migrant worker and his family. This bibliography helps meet the need for those who work with the education of this minority. Covers all areas that relate to migrant labor: monographs, periodicals, pamphlets, government publications, research reports and audio visual materials. Divided in three parts--topic index, main entries and addenda. Easy to use with topic index which directs user to monographs, articles or

audiovisual materials.
2457 annotated entries.   Many relate specifically to
Mexican Americans in their titles; others suggest them.
Must be one of the most complete bibliographies on the migrant laborer even though the publication date was 1965.   Extremely easy to use.   One of the few long bibliographies with
annotations.

249   Poverty and Human Resources Abstracts. 1966- . Bi-
        monthly.   Institute of Labor and Industrial Relations,
        Ann Arbor, Mich.
        Provides abstracts of all subjects dealing with the
title.   Abstracts of books, periodicals, pamphlets, and reports.   Mainly United States but some international.   Typical
issue has entries under topics such as social conditions, social sciences, social change, health and medical care, education, housing, urban and regional planning, and vocational
training.   Each issue divided by topics, then entries placed
under topics.   Extremely useful indexing, by author and by
subject.   Final annual issue has cumulative index.   Single
abstract easy to find because of numbered paragraphs.
        Only one small portion of each issue devoted to Mexi-
can Americans.   In 1973, for example, 18 citations were
listed under Mexican American.   Approximately 150-word abstracts give basic bibliographical data and a description of
the contents.   Highly useful.

250   Proyecto Leer Bulletin. 1968- . Quarterly. Washing-
        ton, D.C., Pan American Union.
        Intended "to identify elementary books and other read-
ing and instructional materials in Spanish for children and
adults appropriate for school and public libraries...."   Meant
as a guide for librarians who have Spanish-speaking patrons.
Generally lists current books, occasionally films and records
also listed.   At times lists publishers and producers.   Issues divided into children's books and adults' books.   Since
issues are very short, no need for an index.   Bulletin no. 6
for 1970 is a cumulative issue covering all previous titles;
no. 7, a cumulative subject list.
        Indispensable for any library with Spanish-speaking
patrons.   The cumulative issue divides books by subject,
gives basic bibliographical data and short descriptive summary.   All titles in Spanish but other information in English.
Apparently a newsletter is issued regularly with pre-selection
listing of new books.   Books do not necessarily have Mexican-
American theme.

251   Quezada, María.   Chicano Resource Materials.   n.p.,
      1970?
      Provides a guide to Chicano materials for participants
of Chicano Study Institutes.   Not confined to holdings of one
institution but extended to include libraries and educational
laboratories.   Monographs divided into subject fields--eco-
nomics-labor, education, art, history, literature, philosophy,
psychology, political science, public health and sociology.
Bibliography and information on resource centers.   Materials
organized by format, e.g., articles, books, audiovisual materials, newspapers, and magazines.   No index.
      474 bibliographical entries usually without annotations.
Quezada offers no guidelines as to materials on Mexico.   For
example, the section on art and history has mainly inclusions
from Mexico that do not relate directly to the Mexican American.   Also the inclusion of Enrique Anderson Imbert's Spanish American Literature: A History, seems somewhat exotic.
Of value is the section on audiovisual aids for it has 47
movies on Mexican Americans.   Lack of index or general
topical arrangement of materials makes use somewhat difficult.

252   Quintana, Helena.   A Current Bibliography on Chicanos,
      1960-1973; Selected and Annotated.   Albuquerque,
      N.M.:   University of New Mexico, 1974.   44p.
      "Up-to-date list of current books [since 1960] on Chi-
canos which can be used by teachers who are in need of supplemental materials."   Only classics published prior to this
date listed also.   Entries alphabetized by author's name.
Also included are a list of periodicals and Chicano publishers
and addresses.   Topical index.
      246 annotated entries each of which in addition to
normal bibliographic information include price and educational
level and subject discipline for which book is suitable.   This
is an excellent bibliography for public school teachers as it
apparently was tailored for their use under the auspices of
the College of Education at UNM.   Scattering of titles on
Mexico not defined in guidelines.

253   Raines, Lester.   The Literature of New Mexico: Se-
      lected Items from Writers and Writings of New Mexi-
      co, 1934.   More New Mexico Writers and Writings,
      1935 [mimeographed].   Las Vegas, N.M.:   New
      Mexico Northern University, 1935?   101p.
      Presents biographical sketches of authors who have

resided in New Mexico and some discussion of their works.
All Anglo authors who were born in the late 19th century and
who resided in and occasionally wrote on New Mexico. Arranged alphabetically by author surname. Lists approximately
100 authors. Eleven of these wrote on themes relating to
Hispanos. Some are famous: Willa Cather, Erna Fergusson,
Mary Austin, etc. This is an amateurish compilation and is
extremely uneven and naive. Yet it does provide background
on authors who write on the Southwest in some of their works.
Because of the only 11 out of 100 in this collection who actually include Chicanos as a subject, one might wonder at its
incorporation into a bibliography on Chicano reference books.
However, since materials on the creative writings concerning Mexican Americans are so scarce, a more liberal judgment is necessary. Probably most of these authors are mentioned and studied in Cecil Robinson's With the Ears of
Strangers: The Mexican in American Literature. Copy evaluated was obtained from Library of Congress.

254 Ramón, Simón Rene. Vocabulario selecto del español
     regional de Del Río, Tejas. Master's thesis. San
     Marcos, Texas: Southwest Texas State University,
     1974. 70p.
     This is another study of the regional Spanish of Texas
done under the auspices of Southwest Texas State University.
It follows the usual format of these studies and includes history, methodology, vocabulary, expressions and bibliography.
The vocabulary has over 250 entries that the author defines
by 12 criteria, including regionalism, variations, definitions,
at times use in context, and a translation of the latter. The
words were selected by listening to the speech of this area
and then including in the study only those words not considered
to be standard Spanish. This study also has 200 regional expressions. Galvan and Teschner incorporated this work into
the Dictionary of the Spanish of Texas.

255 La Raza Yearbook. Los Angeles, n. p. , 1968. (micro-
     film) 76p.
     Intended to show the militant aspects of la raza ac-
cording to various newspapers for the year 1968. "Impres-
sionistic highlights of a whole year of la raza nueva. " Militant poetry, prose, corridos, art, and journalism of certain
Mexican American newspapers in the Southwest. Also contains goals of la raza. Chaotic arrangement with no table
of contents or index.

This composite work indicates the attitudes of the militant wing of chicanismo. It is of reference value for two reasons. Names, addresses and samples of Chicano newspapers are presented. In other words, this could be a guide to militant Chicano newspapers. Of equal value is the collection of documents apparently heterogeneously gathered concerning Chicano rights as related mainly to education but also to the Vietnam war, police power, justice, and the grape strike.

256   Reimer, Ruth (comp.). An Annotated Bibliography of
      Material on Ethnic Problems in Southern California
      [preliminary draft]. Los Angeles: Haynes Foundation
      and Department of Anthropology, University of California, 1947?
      Lists mainly unpublished materials on minority groups in southern California. Japanese, Filipinos, Negroes, Mexican Americans, and Dust Bowl migrants in monographs and journals, mainly 1900 to ca. 1946. Alphabetized by author with subject index that leads to numbered paragraphs.
      Although dated, this is the only bibliography that emphasizes unpublished materials. 376 annotated entries with incisive critical comments. Many entries refer to Mexican Americans. Unfortunately only the holdings of 11 libraries in southern California were surveyed. This work suggests the need for a much broader study that would incorporate the unpublished holdings of university libraries.

257   Resendez, Victor, Jr. Vocabulario español de Seguin,
      Texas. Master's thesis. San Marcos, Texas: Southwest Texas State University, 1970. 81p.
      Resendez presents approximately 420 words and 32 expressions from San Marcos, Texas. These words, selected from interviews with natives, were included only if they varied from standard Spanish. He categorizes each entry by part of speech, definition, use in context, translation of the latter two, and a system of codes to indicate the word's relationship to the Diccionario de la léngua española. This work has value in that it recognizes the Spanish spoken in one small area of Texas. It is included in Galvan's and Teschner's The Dictionary of the Spanish of Texas.

258   Rivera, Feliciano. A Guideline for the Study of the
      Mexican American People in the United States. San

Jose, Cal.:   San Jose State College, 1969.   266p.
This is an attempt to present a true history of the
Mexican American people for teachers and students.   Covers
origin and background of the Mexican people, social and cultural implications in the Southwest after 1850, migration,
contemporary problems and solutions.   A selected bibliography and almost 200 pages of documents.   Arranged in this
order.
This work could be used selectively from junior high
school through college.   The history is presented in an outline form and is apparently meant for the novice.   The bibliography has no guidelines as to selections but has ten pages
of monographs and visual materials on Mexico and the Mexican Americans.   The greater part of the book is made up of
documents.   Unfortunately the two most valuable ones for the
Mexican Americans, i. e., the Treaty of Guadalupe-Hidalgo
and the Constitution of the State of California, are facsimiles
in Spanish and English translations.   Consequently they are
difficult to read.   Yet Rivera's work is valuable for the
school with few resources on Mexican Americans.

259   Rivera, Feliciano.   A Mexican American Source Book
      with Study Guidelines.   Menlo Park, Cal.:   Education-
      al Consulting Associates, 1970.   196p.
Bibliography, missions, illustrations, portfolio of outstanding Americans of Mexican descent, Treaty of Guadalupe
Hidalgo.   In other words, a brief survey of the Mexican
Americans.   In addition to the above, the bibliography has
examples of all genres.   Table of contents but no index.
This work has value mainly for high school students.
It is designed for the library that can afford only representative works on the Mexican American but the scholar would
desire a work with greater scope.   The value of Rivera's
source book is its variety: guidelines of history of Mexican
people in U. S., selected bibliography, missions of California,
a portfolio of illustrations, a portfolio of outstanding Americans of Mexican descent, Treaty of Guadalupe Hidalgo, critical comments on Treaty of Guadalupe Hidalgo, and important
documents from U. S. History.

260   Rivero, E. M. (comp.).   Mexican American Bibliogra-
      phy.   Redlands, Cal.:   University of Redlands, Arma-
      cost Library, 1972.   28p.
Guide to Chicano related materials in the Armacost
Library.   All print materials.   Mexican and Mexican Ameri-

can themes. Monographs, periodical articles, Mexican-American periodicals and newspapers, arranged under these sections by author surname. No index.
224 entries on Mexican and Mexican-American materials, for the most part annotated. Difficult to use because of the lack of an index. Leaves out major bibliographic and other sources of information such as indexes and abstracts and presents no inclusion criteria. Also has no suggestion to the user for researching Mexican-American themes.

261   Robertson, James Alexander. List of Documents in Spanish Archives Relating to the History of the United States Which Have Been Printed or for Which Transcripts Are Preserved in American Libraries. Washington: Carnegie Institution, 1910. 368p.
Provides a guide for scholars who cannot consult the original documents. Includes documents from Spanish archives that relate directly to the United States but does not include decrees and laws found in Recopilación de Leyes de Indias. Divided into two parts, published documents and transcripts. Documents arranged chronologically with date, place, brief description, and printed sources. Transcripts also organized chronologically with date, place of writing, place of conservation of original manuscript, and place of conservation of transcript. 29-page index.
Lists at least 63 entries on California, New Mexico, and Texas.

262   Rocq, Margaret Miller (ed.). California Local History; A Bibliography and Union List of Library Holdings. Stanford, Cal.: Stanford University Press, 1970. 611p.
Designed to make as complete a list as possible of the holdings on Californiana by 177 Californian libraries and 53 out-of-state libraries. Entries from 19th century to 1960. Books and pamphlets, dissertations, and theses. Omitted were: fiction, poetry, cookbooks, natural science, journeys and voyages, juvenile books, newspapers and periodicals. Arranged alphabetically by county, then entries alphabetized under the following categories--county history, register, directories, and general references. Also regional works and California statewide works. Index of authors, personal and place names appearing in titles and some subject entries.
17,261 unannotated entries. Must be the most complete bibliography on Californiana. Although Mexican Ameri-

cans not entered as a subject in the index, innumerable entries relate to this group. As arrangement indicates, geographical approach very easy with this work. Entries give
author, title, publisher, date, and library where book is located.

263 Romero, Philomena. New Mexican Dishes. Los Ala-
      mos, N. M. , n. p. , 1970. 47p.
      A collection of recipes of the New Mexican Hispanos.
Apparently Hispano recipes for all meals. Alphabetically
arranged table of contents.
      No introduction to give scope and definition to Hispano
food of New Mexico. Approximately 75 entries or recipes.
In addition to ingredients gives detailed instructions.

264 Rosen, Carl L. , and Philip D. Ortego. Issues in Lan-
      guage and Reading Instruction of Spanish-Speaking
      Children: An Annotated Bibliography. Newark, Del. :
      International Reading Assoc. , 1971. 31p.
      The purpose of this bibliography is to present a cross-
section of the materials relating to the education and needs
of Spanish speaking children. Mainly articles but also monographs relating to this problem. The materials run from
1953 to ca. 1971. The compilers have arranged their materials under six separate categories: general factors and
underlying issues, measuring and appraising intelligence,
factors pertaining to language development, factors pertaining to reading achievement, bilingual education, and reviews
of research and bibliographies.
      Has approximately 140 prescriptively annotated entries.
This probably is the work's main value, i. e. , it is much
more informational than most bibliographies. It seems
strange, however, that the compilers did not avail themselves
of the ERIC data base. This would have given them innumer-
ably more entries from which to chose. Also this bibliography seems to be mainly print materials. Some important
works were not noted in the section on reviews and bibliographies. Copy examined was obtained from the International
Reading Association Library.

265 Rosen, Pamela, and Eleanor V. Horne. Tests for
      Spanish Speaking Children: An Annotated Bibliography.
      ERIC, 1971. ED 056 084.
      Designed "to list currently available instruments ap-

propriate for use with the Spanish-speaking children," including measures for intelligence, personality, ability and achievement. These instruments were found in Research and Education, the Current Index to Journals in Education, and among the documents in Educational Testing Service. Seems limited to primary grades. Tests entered alphabetically by name.

Lists and evaluates 21 tests of the type described above. Each entry has author, title, name and address of distributor, and most important, a 160-word analysis of the test that includes content, age level of examinees, validity, directions available, types of schools where most effective, and relevance for Spanish-speaking children. This brief bibliography is imperative in any school with Spanish-speaking children. Relevance to Chicanos is obvious. See also Don Hamilton's work.

266 Rowland, Leon. Los Fundadores: Herein Are Listed
     the First Families of California and Also Other Per-
     sons with Family Names That Were in California
     1769-1785 Except Those Who Died at San Diego in
     1769. Fresno: Academy of California Church His-
     tory, 1951.
     "An attempt to list the names of men who came from Mexico to northern California in the first fifteen years of its settlement...." Lists soldados, pobladores, sirvientes, and presidarios taken from the records of seven central Californian missions. The geographical area, "northern California," is not well defined. Names entered alphabetically. This work, although short, has a surname index.
     Approximately 194 Spanish surnames included in this genealogical-type guide. Each name includes basic information: date and place of birth, occupation, year of arrival in California, marriages, spouse and children, and occasionally ethnic background. Besides mission records, Rowland also used other basic sources such as Bancroft and Palou. Excellent for genealogical or historical search of a limited area in California. Very good index.

267 Saldaña, Nancy. Mexican-Americans in the Midwest:
     An Annotated Bibliography. East Lansing: Michigan
     State University, 1969. (Department of Sociology,
     Rural Manpower Center, Special Paper no. 10.) 60p.
     A bibliography of Mexican Americans living in Michigan and other parts of the Midwest and occasionally Texas.

Materials are articles and books, 1920 to 1968.   Bibliography in 14 categories.   Introduction, acculturation, attitudes, demographic analysis, distinctive cultural components, education, employment and income, marriage and family, general discussion, housing, migration and immigration, language, political behavior, and social status.   No index.
     This is one of the best bibliographies.   Each section has entries and then an analytical discussion of these entries suggesting the status of scholarship within a specific area. A total of 125 entries mainly on social science.   Lacking are the fields of folklore and literature.   A thematic and author index would have made this work easier to use.

268   Salinas, Esteban, Ruth M. Bagnall and William Kuvlesky.   Mexican Americans: A Survey of Research by the Texas Agricultural Experiment Station, 1964-1973. ERIC, 1973.   ED 082 913.
     Intended to increase public awareness concerning the research done at the Texas Agricultural Experiment Station on the Mexican American population and to make known these research findings.   Limited to Mexican Americans in Texas in journal articles, papers, reports, and theses.   Mainly of social science orientation.   Arranged by format.
     Over 40 reports listed in this bibliography which diffuses information on items probably never before published. All entries originated at Texas Agricultural Experiment Station.   They contain materials on relocation of Mexican Americans, ambitions, class mobility, school drop-outs, occupational orientation, etc.   This is an example of what every research-oriented school should do to publicize their findings on Mexican Americans.

269   San Bernardino [Cal.] Valley College Library.   Black and Brown Bibliography: History; Literature, Art, Music, Theatre; Philosophy, Social Sciences, Political Science, Education.   San Bernardino: California State College Library, 1970.   3 vols.
     A selective guide to this library's holdings on Negroes and Mexican Americans.   All monographs and in the fields mentioned in the title--divided into three separate volumes. Entries listed unalphabetically under the various topics.   No index.
     751 unannotated entries.   The majority of entries are on blacks.   One wonders about the motive for putting black and brown together in the same bibliography since the user

is generally not interested in both ethnic groups. Also, if
ethnic groups belong together in one bibliography, why the
exclusion of Orientals? No guidelines as to selection. This
bibliography is extremely difficult to use without an index and
with the integration of Chicanos and blacks. Missing also are
periodicals and non-print materials.

270 San Diego [Cal.] Public Library. Chicano: A Selected
    List [mimeographed]. San Diego, Cal.: San Diego
    Public Library, Social Science Section, 1974. 21p.
    A guide to Mexican American materials in the San
Diego Public Library: monographs, some articles, and a
list of periodicals that apparently covers all aspects of Chicanismo. Entries alphabetized under 11 distinct subject
headings. No index.
    Approximately 160 annotated entries. For a library
bibliography this one has several merits. First, it stays
within the limits of the term Mexican American and makes
little effort to include materials from Mexico. It also has
one brief section on the Chicana. Although it establishes
no guidelines, this bibliography presents a good cross-section of Mexican-American materials. Perhaps a later updating will add non-print materials and some of the books
listed in Cecil Robinson's With the Ears of Strangers: The
Mexican in American Literature.

271 Sánchez, George I. Materials Relating to the Education
    of Spanish-Speaking People in the United States. Aus-
    tin: University of Texas, Institute of Latin American
    Studies, 1959. 76p.
    Mainly for Mexicans in the United States but also of
interest to other Spanish-speaking people. Books, articles,
courses of study, bibliographies, and unpublished theses and
dissertations, arranged by the above mentioned formats.
Topical index with cross references.
    882 numbered annotated entries. Earliest date ap-
pears to be approximately 1931. Title is misleading because
books other than education are included--sociology, literature,
and demography. Excellent annotations.

272 Sánchez, Nellie van de Grift. Spanish and Indian Place
    Names of California; Their Meaning and Their Ro-
    mance. San Francisco: A. M. Robertson, 1914.
    446p.

110   Reference Materials

A handbook and a tourist guide to the Spanish and Indian place names of California--apparently only certain areas
and not the entire state. Not an integrated dictionary. Book
divided into chapters on geographical regions and under these
regions the names are listed. No index to lead to geographical name.
     This is not a first choice for a dictionary of Spanish
geographical names for it lacks an index and has no bibliography. Entries have definitions and a short paragraph indicating location and perhaps some historical information.
Pronunciation not offered with word. The work is useful in
the rather indefinable area of pride of heritage.

273 Santa Barbara [Cal.] County Board of Education. The
     Emerging Minorities in America; A Resource Guide
     for Teachers. Santa Barbara, Cal.: ABC-Clio Inc.,
     1972. 256p.
     "Provide[s] assistance in curriculum development
through incorporation into the curriculum of the cultural and
historical contributions of minority groups." Covers Afro
Americans, Asian Americans, Indian Americans and Mexican
Americans. Each cultural group is considered in historical
perspective; has biographical summaries, and bibliography of
print materials. Each cultural group listed separately with
entries under the above divisions.
     The Mexican American section of this resource guide
is 23 pages in length. It contains five pages of historical
perspective; 16 pages on biographical summaries and three
pages of bibliography. The 45 biographical sketches are on
successful Mexican Americans from a variety of fields. They
are historical and contemporary figures. The books for
teachers comprise a basic list of works that might be obtainable in any public library. Unfortunately, this resource
guide, especially because of its California origin, should have
more on Mexican Americans. The disproportion seems
strange, i.e., blacks have 87 pages and Mexican Americans,
23. If this book is meant for high school and junior high
teachers, bibliographies of materials for this age level should
be listed. A 1972 guide with no visual materials is unfor-
giveable.

274 Santos, Richard G. A Preliminary Report on the Ar-
     chival Project in the Office of the County Clerk of
     Bexar County. San Antonio, Texas, 196? 17p.
     Lists the collections of the Bexar County Archives and

also provides a description of contents and a key to the microfilms available.   Earliest entry is 1736.   Arranged in this
order.   Under Spanish Mexican records are land grants and
sales, mission records, lands outside Bexar County, wills
and estates, protocols, etc.   This section has documents
from 1736 to 1836.   Section II is composed of early records
in the office of the county clerk and is mainly 19th century.
        This work is helpful in its listing of archival material.
It is a beginning.   Yet a more detailed study is necessary or
a catalog of the documents.   Many of the collections obviously refer to Mexicans in Texas during the period suggested
above.

275   Saunders, Lyle.   The Education of Spanish American
        and Mexican Children: A Selected Bibliography.   Al-
        buquerque: University of New Mexico, 1944.   4p.
        A guide to readings on education of Mexican-American
children.   In spite of title this bibliography refers mainly to
Mexican Americans.   Few books but mainly articles and
mimeographed materials written between 1928 and 1944.
Divided into bibliography and education.
        50 unannotated entries in English of very short arti-
cles that relate to multiple aspects of education.

276   Saunders, Lyle (comp.).   A Guide to Materials Bear-
        ing on Cultural Relations in New Mexico.   Albuquer-
        que.   University of New Mexico Press, 1944.   528p.
        "An attempt to list ... those published and manuscript
materials having some relevance to problems of cultural relations between the three main ethnic groups within the State
of New Mexico...."   From pre-Spanish period to ca. 1944.
Monographs, articles, and manuscripts.   History, humanities
and social science.   Indian, Spanish and Anglo cultures.   Dic-
tionary-guide and separate supplemental bibliographies of reference works.   Indian cultures, Spanish colonial and Mexican
periods, American frontier period, Spanish-Americans and
Mexicans, etc.   Author and subject indexes.
        One of the most thorough guides to New Mexico print
materials.   Has a total of 5335 entries.   Three sections, the
dictionary guide, Spanish colonial and Mexican period, and
Spanish America and Mexico relate mainly to Mexican Americans.   Approximately 710 unannotated entries in the latter
two sections.   Covers all aspects of Mexican Americans and
also shows their relationship to the other two cultures.   Naturally the work is now dated but is one of the best for the pre-

1944 period.   The compiler, Lyle Saunders, is a skilled bibliographer.

277   Saunders, Lyle.   Spanish-Speaking Americans and Mexi-
         can Americans in the United States: A Selected Bib-
         liography.   Albuquerque: University of New Mexico,
         School of Inter-American Affairs, 1944.   12p.
       A guide to books on the subject which because of "re-
cency, availability, and informative value" would appeal to
classroom teachers.   Mainly Mexican-American but with occasional reference to other Spanish-speaking groups.   Concentrates on the Southwest.   Books, articles, and unpublished
studies dating from 1920 to 1943.   Includes bibliographies,
general, topical section on history, social sciences, education, health, architecture, folklore, etc.
       One of the earliest general bibliographies on Mexican
Americans.   352 unannotated items that relate to multiple
aspects of Mexican Americans.

278   Saunders, Lyle.   The Spanish-Speaking Population of
         Texas.   Austin: University of Texas Press, 1949.
         56p.
       Makes current and refines the census made of the
Spanish-name population in Texas from 1820 to 1948.   First
third of book is a definition of terms, a summary of the
activities of the Bureau of Census among the Mexican Americans, and a synthesis of the distribution of this population in
Texas.   Remainder of book tables and maps.
       Must be one of early attempts to refine statistics
about Mexican Americans.   Tables show ratios of Mexican
Americans to Anglos by entire state, by counties, by school
enrollment.

279   Sax, Antimaco.   Los mexicanos en el destierro.   San
         Antonio, Texas,   n. p. , 1916.   179p.
       Designed to make known what exile is and what the
Mexican exiles have done in the United States since the fall
of Victoriano Huerta.   Includes biographies of the most important exiles living in the United States.   Divided into three
parts: Emigration and the emigrants, biographical notes,
and viewpoints of the emigrants.   Has table of contents but
no index.
       This is a very biased work written by a sympathizer
of the Huerta regime.   It has some reference value, however,

in the second section, "Biographical Notes." Writing in
Spanish, Sax gives biographical sketches of important exiles.
He notes mainly what they had done in Mexico and focuses
on their survival in the United States. He ignores typical
biographical data. His work is one of the few on the Mexicans as temporary residents in the U.S. It fills in a neglected area of Mexican American studies and for this reason is useful.

280 Schmidt, Fred H. Spanish Surnamed American Employ-
     ment in the Southwest: A Study Prepared for the Colo-
     rado Civil Rights Committee under the Auspices of the
     Equal Employment Opportunity Commission. Washing-
     ton, D. C.: U. S. Gov. Printing Office, 1970? 247p.
     Provides statistical information on job patterns of
Spanish surnamed individuals from 1940 to 1966. Has 80
pages of text and statistics on employment of Spanish surnamed, i.e., white collar occupations, training programs,
etc., and a brief history of these people and Anglo attitudes
toward them. Arranged in two sections. First part as described above; the final 162 pages contain charts on employment patterns with the majority of charts on employment patterns for industry in selected counties. Summarized history
of Chicano employment in the Southwest.

281 Schramko, Linda Fowler. Chicano Bibliography: Se-
     lected Materials on Americans of Mexican Descent.
     Sacramento, Cal.: Sacramento State College Library,
     1970. 124p.
     Brings together Chicano materials available at Sacra-
mento State College. Education, health and psychology, historical background, literature and fine arts, social life, Chicano periodicals, and guide to further information. Monographs, articles, and microfilms. Entries by author under
categories mentioned. Subject index but no author index.
     1000 unannotated entries. No explanation for selec-
tion or non-selection of works from Mexico. Most valuable
section is that on education which is divided into social and
cultural aspects, psychology and guidance, teachers and teaching, and special project. The section on literature and fine
arts has too many entries from Mexico.

282 Scott, William H. O. Spanish-Speaking Americans: A
     Bibliography of Government Documents. Bellingham:

Western Washington State College, Wilson Library,
1972. 7p.
A guide to government documents on the above topic
in the Wilson Library. Covers agriculture, commerce, civil
rights, civil service, General Services Administration, Health,
Education and Welfare, Supreme Court, Labor, Commissions
and Committees, and Washington State Government documents.
35 entries. Easy to use because of the subdivision
and the listing of the standard call numbers for government
documents. Entries refer mainly to Mexican Americans and
also to Puerto Ricans but other entries on minorities in general, e. g., Directory for Reaching Minority Groups. This
looks like a complete listing of recent government documents
especially if used with the two other bibliographies previously
sponsored by the Wilson Library--Chicanos: A Bibliography
of Government Documents (see under Mignon, Molly) and Migrant Labor: A Bibliography of Pamphlets and Government
Publications in Wilson Library, both by Molly Mignon. These
guides are valuable because their entries are probably in any
library that is a U. S. Government depository.

283 Seattle Public Library. Chicano Bibliography. Seattle,
     1973. 7p.
     Guide to the Mexican-American monograph holdings of
the Seattle Public Library. Mainly works dealing with Mexican Americans, with only an occasional title on Mexico. Alphabetized by author with all topics integrated into one list.
     Approximately 112 unannotated entries, each with call
number, author, title, and subject field. No criteria for selection presented.

284 Segreto, Joan (comp.). Bibliografía: A Bibliography on
     the Mexican American. Houston, Texas: Houston In-
     dependent School District, 1970. 25p. ED 046 616
     Sources to help teachers increase their knowledge of
Mexican Americans. Divided into the following sections: another perspective on America; the arts; literature, music,
art, dances; heritage; history; Mexican-American life today;
additional bibliographies; periodicals and newspapers.
     This bibliography has over 100 unannotated items. It
reflects the attitudes of the late '60s in that it has no introduction nor does it distinguish between Mexico and the Mexican
American. Perhaps the most original section is distinguished
personalities, but here again the list is flawed by the inclusion of Mexicans. This work has value for the small high

school and public library.   Yet surely many annotated bibliographies now supersede it.

285   Shepherd, William R. Guide to the Materials for the
      History of the United States in Spanish Archives (i.e.,
      Simancas, the Archivo Histórico Nacional, and Se-
      ville.) Washington, D.C.: Carnegie Institution, 1907.
      107p.
      A guide to manuscripts relating to continental United
States in three Spanish archives.   16th century to ca.1850.
Materials refer to New Spain, the Caribbean, and the United
States, i.e., Florida, Louisiana, Texas, New Mexico, and
California.   Arranged by archive and then enumeration of
documents.   Eight-page name index.
      At least 53 entries relating to the southwestern United
States.   No details of contents of documents, just a broad
description.   Topics include colonization, boundaries, cor-
respondence for governors, maps, etc.

286   Slobodek, Mitchell.   A Selective Bibliography of Cali-
      fornia Labor History.   Los Angeles: University of
      California, Institute of Industrial Relations, 1964.
      265p.
      A guide to the literature of labor history of California.
Publications date from mid-19th century to ca.1962.   However, period encompassed goes back to Spanish California.
Monographs and journals, magazines and newspaper articles.
Entries alphabetized under topics--Spanish and Mexican backgrounds; industries, crafts, and trades; white collar groups;
special groups; national and racial minorities, etc.   Subject
and author index.
      Two sections of this bibliography pertain to Mexican
Americans--Spanish and Mexican background and national and
racial minorities.   This is a total of 78 partially annotated
entries.   Other references to Mexican Americans would have
to be sought under specific industries such as agriculture.
Other classifications such as labor legislation and labor market would prove useful to the scholar on Mexican American labor in California.   Had the author done a more thorough job
of indexing and cross referencing, the bibliography would have
been more useful.   For example, the index has no entries under migrant.

287   Smith, Jessie Carney.   Minorities in the United States:

Guide to Resources. Nashville, Tenn. : Peabody Library School, 1973. 133p. ED 080 133
"It is intended as ... a guide for librarians, library school students, library schools, other educators, and other students ... interested in bibliographic and other resources for the study of various minorities. " Native Americans, Blacks, Asiatics, Puerto Ricans, and Mexican Americans. All print materials. Arranged by ethnic group and then citations entered alphabetically under topics.

Approximately 180 unannotated entries on the Mexican American in monographs and journals. Many are casually selected monographs on Mexico. Although this bibliography provides rather standard entries, it is commendable for the following reasons. In the prefatory remarks are listed the major Chicano collections in the United States. The first two pages refer mainly to articles concerning library services and the Chicano, a topic completely ignored in most other bibliographies.

288   Sorvig, Ralph W. A Topical Analysis of Spanish Loan-Words in Written American English of the American Southwest. Ph. D. dissertation, University of Denver, 1952. 295p.

Designed "to collect, to classify, and to analyze, from a cultural point of view, Spanish loan-words found in written American English materials relating to the American Southwest. " Sources date from 1840 to 1950 and include almost 200 works. "Southwest" refers mainly to New Mexico, southern Colorado, and west Texas. Words are alphabetized under nine separate topics such as flora and fauna, trade and transportation, etc. Has table of contents and index with all words listed.

Approximately 1140 words divided into 12 separate categories: topography, flora and fauna, architecture and buildings, domestic arrangement, trade and transportation, mining, cattle, government, church and state, and miscellaneous items. These are all taken from 200 written sources. Each entry with definition, source, i. e. , author and page number, location in technical or general works, Mexican or American Spanish. All sections have introductory pages. Mainly nouns. Author should have presented words in context. One of the few dictionaries that relies totally on written sources. Excellent introduction on loan words.

289   Southern Baptist Church. Home Mission Board. Home

Mission Board: Personnel Directory, 1974-1975. Atlanta: The Board, 1974? 31p.
Directory of the missionary activities of the Southern Baptist Church within the United States. Includes administration and personnel addresses by states. Has index of missionary workers and where they serve.
The pertinent section to the Mexican American is the personnel addresses by states. Alphabetized by state. Under each state is a section labeled language missions, which gives name of mission worker and by abbreviation, the language used in the mission. Many of the entries especially in the Southwest are in Spanish.

290   Southwest Network. Directorio Chicano. Hayward, Cal.: Southwest Network, 1973. 16p.
An attempt to list alternative schools, distribution centers and publications for Chicanos who are seeking identity; based on inquiries made in October and November of 1973. Lists schools, distributing centers, and publications for California, Oregon, Arizona, Colorado, New Mexico, Texas, Illinois, Iowa, Michigan, Minnesota, Missouri, Wisconsin, New York, and Washington, D.C. Arranged in that order, i.e., by geographical region.
Gives names and addresses of institutions and publications of liberal Chicanismo. Although there is only a brief introduction, it does convey the ideas of militancy, e.g., "search for identity uncovered by expounding awareness of a smothered past...." Important as a source for materials. The editors of this directory apparently hope to update the contents periodically.

291   Southwestern Cooperative Educational Laboratory, Inc. Human Resources Center Directory. Albuquerque, N.M., 1971. 108p.
A "reference bank of persons with expertise in educational, socio-economic and cultural matters as they relate to the non-English speaking Spanish surnamed adult." Experts of both Spanish surname and non Spanish surname living in the United States. Major fields of expertise are education, community development, cultural awareness, historical significance of cultures, contemporary problems, and the culture of poverty. Arranged alphabetically by surname of expert. Index lists experts by area of expertise.
648 professionals named who could serve as resource people for the Mexican American. Education subdivided to

adult basic education, English as second language, reading,
writing, math, citizenship, G.E.D., curriculum development,
behavioral objectives, counseling and guidance programs, administration, vocational education and bilingual education.
Each entry with address, present occupation, academic background, expertise, and assignment preference. Important
guide for individuals or institutions who need a consultant.
A geographical index might have facilitated use.

292   Southwestern Historical Quarterly.   Cumulative Index,
      vols. 1-40, and 41-60.   Austin: Texas State Histor-
      ical Association, vol. I, 1950; vol. II, 1960.
      A cumulative index to all issues of the Southwestern
Historical Quarterly, 1897 to 1957.   The publication indexed
has articles, notes, documents, and book reviews on the
Southwest but mainly on Texas.   Integrated subject, topic,
author, title and book titles index.
      Many references in the index are to Mexican Ameri-
cans and Mexico.   La raza can be found under this topic or
under surname, labor, city or county, missions, race and
racial groups, Catholic church, folklore, etc.   In other words,
the two indexes provide guides to 60 volumes of history of
Texas and the Southwest.   Most important continuous journal
on Texas history.

293   Spell, Lota M.   Research Materials for the Study of
      Latin America at the University of Texas.   Austin:
      University of Texas Press, 1954.   107p.
      Notes the development of the Latin American Collec-
tion and provides information on scope, variety, and location of research materials in its eight fields.   Divided into
11 chapters: first three relate to developments of the collection, manuscripts and transcripts and bibliography; the eight
others to various subject disciplines.   Author and subject index.
      Although dated, this work is a valuable guide to the
Latin American Collection.   Almost all sections list works
that relate to Mexican Americans.

294   Spencer, Mima (comp.).   Bilingual Education for Span-
      ish-Speaking Children: An Abstract Bibliography.   Ur-
      bana, Ill.:   ERIC Clearinghouse on Early Childhood
      Education, 1974.   45p.   ED 091 075
      This is another bibliography based on ERIC microfiche

cards. It contains 86 document and journal references in
Research in Education and in Current Index to Journals in
Education. According to the document résumé, the references
relate to programs, issues, materials, and methodology in
bilingual education.
   As in most ERIC publications this one has abstracts
of approximately 150 words. Not only is this bibliography
new, but it includes quite recent publications and reports.
Orientation seems to be mainly to the primary grades.

295 Stanford University. The Mexican American: A Se-
     lected and Annotated Bibliography. 1969. 139p.
   Guide for specialists and laymen to 274 works on contemporary problems of the Mexican American. Books and
articles relating to Mexican Americans with a heavy emphasis
on social science. Also works on poverty and segregation
but no mention of novels. No subdivisions by genre or topic
but subject index. All entries by author but no author index.
   Few entries but well annotated, i. e. , they are generally of abstract length and are often prescriptive. Commendable also are the limits of this work for its entries on
Mexico are mainly studies that relate directly to Mexican
Americans, e. g. , D'Antonio, William V. and William H.
Forn, Influentials in Two Border Cities: A Study in Community Decision Making. This is one of the few Chicano
bibliographies that offers guidelines and also a note on terminology.

296 Stanford University. Center for Latin American Studies.
     The Mexican American: A Selected and Annotated
     Bibliography, 2d. ed. Editor: Luis G. Nogales.
     Stanford, Cal. : Stanford University, 1971, c1969.
     162p.
   Updates the 1969 bibliography with 200 additional annotations. Emphasis is on scholarly publications on Mexican
Americans. Topic is Mexican American but also includes
general works such as authoritarian personality. Mainly monographs arranged alphabetically by author. No subject subdivision but subject and field indexes.
   444 well annotated entries on books, reports and articles. Criteria are too broad for general works could apply
to any human being. Good fiction ignored. Nevertheless,
one of the best bibliographies available and surely one of the
best indexed.

297   Stewart, Eloisa Delgado de.   El Plato Sabroso.   Santa
      Fe, N. M. :   Ortiz Printing Shop, 1972.   20p.
      A recipe book of Hispano recipes of New Mexico; also
one page of menus.   Recipes not alphabetized but brevity of
book permits rapid finding.
      Apparently a popular book because now (1974) in its
13th printing.   Unfortunately the introduction gives no guidance
as to the reason for the selection of the recipes or how the
Hispano food of New Mexico differs from Mexico and the
areas of Mexican concentration in the U. S.   Titles in Spanish with English translation; however, ingredients and directions totally in English.   Probably not the best single source
for Hispano food.

298   Stockton and San Joaquin [Cal.] County Public Library.
      Mexican Americans [mimeographed].   Stockton and
      San Joaquin County, Cal. , 1973.   7p.
      Lists only a portion of the monographs and films re-
lating to the Mexican American in the Stockton and San Joaquin
County Library.   Covers Mexico and Mexican Americans in
the social sciences, history, art, and literature.   Entries
alphabetized under historical topics or subject disciplines.
Shortness of work precludes need for index.
      This is a bibliography for one library.   One wonders
why it should represent just a portion of the collection on
Mexican Americans.   The bibliographical information on the
entries is incomplete with only author, title, and call number.   However, the fiction is annotated.   This guide useful
only to the casual user of the collection.   As in many Chicano bibliographies, no inclusion criteria established.

299   Strange, Susan, and Rhea Pendergrass Priest.   Bibli-
      ography: The Mexican American in the Migrant La-
      bor Setting.   East Lansing: Michigan State University,
      Rural Manpower Center, 1968.   27p.   ED 032 188
      As title suggests, citations relate to the Mexican Amer-
ican in a migrant labor setting.   Materials run from 1928 to
1967 and are grouped under: cultural characteristics, education, employment, health, migrant farm labor, minorities,
minority groups in America, social change and adjustment,
social welfare and youth.   Materials under each subject arranged by format, i. e. , books and articles, reports, proceedings, and theses.
      275 entries with occasional annotations.   Well organ-
ized into the various subject divisions listed above.   However,

compilers offer no guidelines as to selection or non selection
of materials.   Also they offer no reason as to sporadic annotations of entries.   This work should be used with Beverly
Fodell's (q. v.).

300 Talbert, Robert Harria. Spanish-Name People in the
     Southwest and West; Socio-economic Characteristics
     of White Persons of Spanish Surname in Texas, Ari-
     zona, California, Colorado, and New Mexico. Fort
     Worth: Leo Potishman Foundation, Texas Christian
     University, 1955. 90p.
     Intended "to present in usable form much of the sta-
tistical information contained in the 1950 U. S. Census of
Population and Housing [and] to make the available statistical
data understandable to the layman. " Covers geographical and
age distribution, nativity, education, marital status, economic status, and housing of the five states mentioned.   Arranged in this order but with more subdivisions.   Table of
contents and abbreviated index but no guide to tables.
     Though now dated this statistical survey with text pre-
sents valuable data.   Refines the term Mexican American to
mean Spanish Americans or those of colonial derivation, Mexican Americans or those of Mexican parentage but U. S. citizenship, and finally those of recent immigration to the U. S.
Has easy-to-read graphs that present material on employment, education, location, etc.   Study admits defects in statistical gathering by the use of only Spanish surnames and
an office rather than a field survey.   Deficient though the
study may be, it is highly useful and possibly the only source
for statistics on Mexican Americans for 1950.

301 Talbot, Jane Mitchell and Gilbert R. Cruz. A Compre-
     hensive Chicano Bibliography, 1960-1972. Austin,
     Texas: Jenkins Pub. Co. , 1973. 375p.
     Makes available to the researcher a list of publica-
tions about the Mexican American.   Dates as indicated in
title.   Monographs, journal articles, government documents,
dissertations, theses, and audiovisual materials.   Divided
into 20 topical sections, e. g. , history, literature, education,
etc.   Detailed table of contents.   Authors and topical index
leading to numbered entries.
     This is apparently an expanded and improved revision
of A General Bibliography for Research etc. (see following
entry).   The revised version has 4167 unannotated entries.
Although this work is quite easy to use, an index with more

topics would have aided, e.g., there is no mention of regions
or states in index.   Also the introduction does not clarify the
problem of the relationship between Mexico and the Mexican
American.   Consequently, the selection of some Mexican entries over others seems capricious.   Best for researcher interested in post 1960's.   For depth, however, Pino's work
would have to complement this.

302   Talbot, Jane Mitchell, and Gilberto R. Cruz.   A Gen-
       eral Bibliography for Research in Mexican American
       Studies: The Decade of the Sixties to the Present.
       Edinburg, Texas: Pan American University, 1972.
       unpaged.
       Covers books and articles for any serious research
and is highly inclusive: besides traditional categories, also
has church, folklore, and children's literature.   Entries arranged alphabetically by subject.   Topic index only but cross
referenced.
       3155 numbered, unannotated entries.   Probably only
bibliography that has short, specific time limits.   Actually
needs a more refined index.

303   Tash, Steven, and Karin Nupoll (comps.).   La Raza:
       A Selective Bibliography of Library Resources.   North-
       ridge: California State University, 1973.   300p.
       In order to better serve the community, indicates the
holdings of the University Library on the Mexican and Mexican American in books, periodicals, articles, filmstrips,
government documents and microforms.   Arranged according to Library of Congress list of subject headings.   24 separate categories, e.g., reference materials, agricultural
labor, Chicano life style, Mexico, religion, etc.   Table of
contents and personal name index.
       3173 sporadically annotated entries with minimal bib-
liographical information and call numbers.   These entries
fall into three large categories--Mexicans, Mexican Americans, and general sources.   The latter refers to books on
prejudice, delinquency, the exceptional child, etc.   This bibliography seems complete and easy to use.   A longer introduction should have been provided to describe the criteria
for inclusion.   Commendable is the presence of entries on
Steinbeck and Willa Cather, authors normally ignored in bibliographies of this nature.   Each of 24 categories divided into two sections--reference resources and general resources.
On the whole excellent.

304   Taylor, Virginia H.   The Spanish Archives of the Gen-
      eral Land Office of Texas.   Austin, Texas: Lone
      Star Press, 1955.   258p.
      "Present[s] a concise descriptive and chronological
narrative which will serve as a composite picture for those
who are interested in both the history and content of these
archives."   Origin of land titles in Texas, land grants made
by Spain in Texas, the Texas vara, Spanish and Mexican
grants between the Nueces River and the Rio Grande, Spanish
and Mexican grants in Chihuahua, Republic and State of Texas,
and special disposition of titled lands between Nueces River
and Rio Grande.   Titles granted before 1836; arranged in
this order.   Also has subject index.
      Apparently one of few works dealing with Spanish and
Mexican land grants in Texas.   Titles to these grants are
the bases of ownership for 26 million acres of land in Texas.
Of special value is the appendix, which lists 4200 original
grantees, giving name and date of title, amount, colony or
commissioner, and present location.   Many of the grantees
have Spanish surnames.

305   Teschner, Richard V. (comp.).   Spanish-Surnamed Pop-
      ulation of the United States; A Catalog of Dissertations.
      Ann Arbor, Mich. :   University Microfilms.   43p.
      Lists all dissertations relating to the Spanish surnamed
in the U. S. :   Cubans, Mexican Americans and Puerto Ricans.
Taken from Comprehensive Dissertation Index, 1861-1972.
Arranged by discipline: social sciences, education, humanities, and sciences.   Alphabetical under these divisions.   Author index.
      1197 unannotated entries with author, title, university,
year, and number of pages; 391 entries directly relate to
Mexican Americans.   Largest number of dissertations on
Mexican Americans in single list.   Dissertations usually scat-
tered in with published works and journal articles in other
bibliographies.

306   Texas Education Agency.   Social Studies Section.   Books
      on the Mexican American; A Selected Listing.   Austin?,
      n. p. , 1972.   13p.
      Designed to assist social science instructors and li-
brarians in selecting and obtaining books on Mexican Americans.   Solely monographs of a social science orientation and
mainly for secondary and junior high schools.   Listed alphabetically under two main sections, books for students and

books for teachers. Also list of book publishers.
Has 67 descriptively annotated entries, mainly Mexican American selections but occasionally a title from Mexico.
Very traditional books on Mexican Americans and no suggested bibliographies to augment this list. Some of the selections on Mexico are probably too advanced for high school
level. The brief introduction to this bibliography establishes
no guidelines or inclusion criteria and the section on books
for teachers includes several pejorative works on the Mexican Americans. Much effort should be spent to upgrade this
bibliography and make it reflective of a state with a large
number of Mexican Americans.

307   Texas Education Agency.   Social Studies Section.   The
      Treatment of Minorities; Guidelines for Selecting Text-
      book Materials.   Austin: The Agency, Div. of Pro-
      gram Development, 1973. 5p.
      A list of criteria and suggested aids for choosing ma-
terials on minorities mainly for high school and junior high.
Presents list of guidelines, a suggested evaluation form for
books, and suggested references.
      An indispensable reference for teachers who wish to
incorporate ethnic material into their present curriculum.
Probably meant for grades 6-12; however, could with varia-
tion also apply to K-6 and college for the validity of the
guidelines. This reference intended mainly for print materials but could also apply to audiovisual materials. Two of
the six suggested references apply specifically to Mexican
Americans.

308   Texas Institute for Educational Development.   The Chi-
      cano Almanac.   Austin: Futura Press, 1973.   242p.
      Information about Texas Chicanos in a useful form.
Data gathered since 1970 from many sources. Covers 67
counties of Texas whose populations are at least 25 percent
Chicano. Arranged alphabetically by county. Each county
with the same format for information.
      An attempt to abstract scattered information on Texas
Chicanos. Includes business, economics, and general geographic information. Population characteristics, county
health information, education, county income characteristics
and also educational systems. Easy-to-read format. This
book is based on 11 previous studies.

309   Texas State Library.   Handbook: Texas Archival and
       Manuscript Depositories, compiled by James Day.
       Austin: Texas Library and Historical Commission,
       1966. 73p.
       Brief description of the archives throughout the state
of Texas. Also lists institutions without archives and those
not reporting. For those reporting, this description includes
--staff, hours of operation, reproduction equipment, size,
type and content of holdings and published guides. Arranged
alphabetically by locality, then by institution.
       Ostensibly, the cities with materials relevant to Mexi-
can Americans are Austin, El Paso, Houston, Nacogdoches,
and San Antonio.

310   Tibón, Gutierre.   Diccionario etimológico comparado de
       nombres proprios de personas.   Mexico City: Tal-
       lares de Editorial Fournier, 1956. 565p.
       An attempt to explore the origins and meanings of first
names used in the Hispanic world. Names from the Christian
calendar, mythology, history, literature and indigenous heroes
of America.
       Approximately 5580 given names that occur in the His-
panic world. Each entry with national origin of name, variations, and historical person who carried the name. Several
books relate to family names, but this is the only work in
this bibliography devoted to given names. Lists many of the
names used among Mexican Americans. Unique and useful
and definitely a Chicano reference book.

311   Tibón, Gutierre.   Onomástica hispanoamericana.   Mexi-
       co City: Tallares de la Editorial Intercontinental,
       1961. 360p.
       Guide to certain family and given names that occur in
Spain and the Americas. Names are of Spanish, Italian,
French, Jewish, Arabic, and Mexican Indian origin. 33 chapters on names often omitted from the usual onomastic dictionaries. Indexes of family and given names and indexes of
place names.
       This work is not as useful as Tibón's Diccionario
etimológico comparado (see preceding entry); however, Onomástica hispanoamericana does fulfill the need mentioned
above, i. e., to trace the more unusual names in the Hispanic cultures. Of importance to the Mexican American, this
study devotes five chapters to Indian names in Mexico. Discusses prevalence of the name Garza in Monterrey. Excellent index that lists 25,000 names.

312 Toward a Chicano/Raza Bibliography: Drama, Prose,
     Poetry. Berkeley, Cal.: Quinto Sol Publications,
     1973. (El Grito Book Series, no. 2.)
     The compilation of a bibliography of previously uncol-
lected Chicano materials and an attempt to rectify earlier
haphazardly done bibliographies appear to be the goals of
this work. Entries taken from "Chicano journals, newspapers, bulletins and newsletters published in the Southwest by
Chicanos...." Entries by authors under three separate categories: drama, prose, and poetry. No index.
     A very necessary and belated bibliography on Chicano
creative writing. The only other work of this nature is a bibliography by Carlota Cárdenas de O'Dwyer (q. v.). The importance of the El Grito bibliography is its listing of many previously
uncollected items. Has 85 entries in prose, 15 in drama,
and 1410 in poetry. In the short introduction, the compiler
gives no definition of Chicano literature. Apparently it is
any type of literature created by Chicanos.

313 Trejo, Arnulfo D. Algunos Libros by and about Mexi-
     can Americans. Tucson: University of Arizona Li-
     brary, 1971. 23p.
     Intended "to identify at least a small portion of the
Mexican-American collection ... of the University of Arizona."
Guides and index, bibliography, biography, background surveys, social sciences, and humanities, arranged in this order.
All print materials.
     138 annotated entries on a cross-section of the Chi-
cano holdings at the University of Arizona. Very good basic
guide that lists the major bibliographies and includes also fiction of Anglos on Chicanos, e. g., J. Frank Dobie. Trejo
also guides the reader to the major sources of Anglo works, e. g.
Cecil Robinson's With the Ears of Strangers, probably the
best analysis of the Mexican in American literature. The
compiler has not diluted his work by incorporating materials
on Mexico that do not relate directly to the Mexican American. The only defect is the absence of major indexes and
abstracts.

314 Trejo, Arnulfo D. (ed.). Directory of Spanish-Speak-
     ing/Spanish-Surnamed Librarians in the United States.
     Tucson: University of Arizona, College of Education,
     Bureau of Educational Research and Services, 1972.
     (School of Library Science Paper, no. 3.) 15p.
     "Give[s] visibility to the names of librarians in this

country who, because of language and/or culture identify with
Spanish-speaking Americans. " Covers librarians of the a-
bove description. Ten different Spanish-speaking nationalities
are included. Arranged alphabetically by surname. Approximately 225 librarians listed along with addresses and libraries;
61 are Mexican Americans. Although title encompasses Spanish-speaking librarians, few Anglo names are included. Main
source was the 1970 Biographical Directory of Librarians in
the United States and Canada and personal contacts of compilers.
      The updated edition of the above appeared in 1973 and
includes names of 320 professional librarians who are either
of Spanish origin or are Spanish speaking. More refinement
of ethnic diversity is visible in this updated directory, for
in addition to the librarians of Spanish and Spanish American
origin, the revision also includes Anglo Americans and other
European nationalities. The 1973 updated directory is much
improved over and much less biased than the first.

315   Trejo, Francisco. Chicano Bibliography. Minneapolis:
      Minneapolis Public Schools, Task Force on Ethnic
      Studies, 1972. 13p. ED 076 475
      Although no purpose is stated, this apparently is a
bibliography for use in the Minneapolis Public Schools. Covers books, journals and dissertations from 1938 to 1971.
Entries are alphabetized by authors under special topics,
such as high school materials, history of Mexico, literature,
philosophy, political science, pre-Columbian history, sociology, Southwest history, Chicano journals and articles and
reference materials.
      150 unannotated entries mainly of a social science
orientation. A fair cross-section but very weak in creative
literature, both by Anglos and Chicanos. The citations from
Mexico are casually selected. An educational institution
should provide guidelines for searching for this topic in the
library, i.e., subject headings and useful indexes and abstracts.

316   Trueba, Henry T. Mexican American Bibliography.
      Bilingual Bicultural Education. ERIC, 1973. 26p.
      ED 085 120
      Guide to 306 books and articles on Mexican Americans
and bilingual education. Has bibliographies, biculturalism,
bilingual education, economics, sociology, etc., between 1919
and 1973. Arranged into three major sections: social sci-

ences, education, and bibliographies.   No index or table of contents.

This bibliography provides quite a good cross section and could be useful for secondary and junior high level. However, none of the entries is annotated and the author provides no guidelines for his inclusions.   Like many other bibliographies, this one capriciously selects items from Mexico.

317   Trujillo, Luis M.   Diccionario del Español del Valle
       de San Luis de Colorado y del Norte de Nuevo Mexico.
       Master's thesis, Adams State College, Alamosa, Col.,
       1961.   41p.
       Collects words and phrases used in el Valle de San Luis de Colorado and northern New Mexico and not found in the dictionary of the Spanish Academy.   Limited to the geographical area mentioned above.

Approximately 1248 entries, each with spelling, definition in English, and a symbol indicating if word is a colloquialism, a localism, has suffered phonetic change, retains ancient forms, is an English word hispanicized, a Spanish word anglicized, or is a Mexicanismo.   No use in context or pronunciation provided.   Bibliography included.

318   Tucson [Ariz.] Public Schools.   The Mexican American:
       A Resource Unit.   Part II, Biographical Sketches,
       prepared by Intermediate Grades History and Human
       Relations Committee [mimeographed].   1971.   46p.
       Apparently the main purpose is an attempt to use Mexican-American biographical sketches as an inspiration for teaching in the intermediate grades.   Has Tucsonans of Mexican ancestry, both 19th and 20th centuries, who achieved success in a variety of fields.   The eight brief biographies are in alphabetical order.

These eight biographical sketches are very definitely intended for the elementary and intermediate grades.   As a reference work, the book is mainly of value for grade schools and public libraries.   The eight Mexican Americans are either famous historically or somehow prominent today.   Work has value also as a teaching aid for teachers in Mexican American areas.   Each sketch is followed by useful exercises based upon the text.

319   Tully, Marjorie F., and Juan B. Rael.   An Annotated
       Bibliography of Spanish Folklore in New Mexico and

Southern Colorado.   Albuquerque: University of New
Mexico Press, 1950.   124p.
A guide to literature of folklore for those interested
in the Southwest.   Contains published books and articles,
1900's to 1948, in Spanish and English on any aspect of folklore for this region.   No theses or dissertations.   Author
restricted entries to materials in the libraries at Stanford
and Berkeley.   Arranged alphabetically in one list.   Subject
index leads to numbered paragraphs.
702 full bibliographic entries on topic of folklore,
many with descriptive annotations.   Very useful is the list
of references to reviews about certain of the entries on books.
It would have been helpful had the compilers defined the meaning of "folklore."

320   Turner, Pearl, Ken Karr and Gloria Jameson.   The
Education of Mexican American Children and Teaching
English as a Second Language: Materials Available in
California State Polytechnic College Library.   San
Luis Obispo, Cal., 1969.   18p.
A cross section of materials on (a) the Mexican American and (b) English as a second language.   Mainly print materials but also ERIC documents on microfilm.   Materials on
Mexico, Mexican American, language and education; Children's
books, curriculum materials, textbooks, periodicals, documents, and ERIC materials, arranged in this order.   No index.
540 unannotated entries.   This bibliography has no
stated guidelines to direct the user.   The selections on Mexico seem whimsical and those on Mexican Americans include
no bibliographies.   Of value is the large number of entries
on teaching English and theories of language.   One of the few
bibliographies that lists textbooks.   Of value also are the
children's books on Mexican Americans.   An index would
have made this work more useful.

321   Twitchell, Ralph Emerson (comp.).   The Spanish Archives of New Mexico.   2 vols.   Cedar Rapids, Iowa:
Torch Press, 1914.
A guide to the archives of New Mexico in the Office
of the Surveyor-General of Santa Fe and the Library of Congress; an inventory of documents from 1621 to 1845.   The
first volume describes the New Mexico archives in Santa Fe;
the second, those in the Library of Congress.   Entries are
chronological, with access through name index.

The two volumes together contain over 3000 entries
and annotations. These vary from a few words to several
pages. Each has date, place of occurrence and description.
No mention of number of documents, size, location or condition. Yet author achieved his purpose: "this work has
been arranged with the view of demonstrating that even a
catalog may be interesting as well as profitable reading. "

322   United Presbyterian Church in the United States of
      America. The Program Agency. Directory of Latino
      Pastors of the United Presbyterian Church in the
      U. S. A. [and Puerto Rico] [xerox]. New York: Mis-
      sion Service Unit on Church and Race, 1974. 14p.
      Guide to Spanish-surnamed pastors of this church.
Names of pastors, active or retired, and addresses. For
Puerto Rico also given are candidates for the ministry and
ministers without congregations. Arranged alphabetically by
area. Although states with large Spanish-surname populations
are listed separately, other states are combined into synods.
      Actually in two parts--the United States, and then
Puerto Rico as a supplement. Very short directory, so no
need of index. Gives basic information as stated above.

323   U. S.   Agency for International Development. Spanish-
      Language Film Catalog, 1969-1970 (Catalogo de Peli-
      culas en Español, 1969-1970. Washington, D. C. :
      Agency for International Development, 1969. 213p.
      ED 041 497
      An annotated catalog of 16mm films in Spanish. Cov-
ers multitude of topics: business management; child development; dental hygiene; education; family planning; health; industrial safety; labor; metal work; sanitation; self-help; and
teaching. Divided into seven sections: how to use catalog,
instructions for handling films, how to borrow films, how to
buy films, section index, index of sources, and topic index.
      Although dated now, this is a useful guide to films in
Spanish. Each film is described in Spanish and English with
title, language used, availability and a descriptive annotation.
Does not specifically list Mexican-American topics but general topics of universal interest on practical topics such as
insect enemies, freezing fruits and vegetables, breeding
chickens, etc.

324   U. S.   Cabinet Committee on Opportunities for the Span-

ish Speaking. Directory of Spanish Speaking Community Organizations, June, 1970. Washington, D.C.:
U.S. Gov. Printing Office, 1970. 231p.
   A guide to 207 Spanish-speaking groups from the entire United States. 800 groups contacted for survey but only
207 responded. Mainly citizens' groups involved in the community; profit-making organizations excluded. First lists
national organizations, then by state and city. Subject index.
   Each organization with address, telephone, principal
officers, scope, date established, ethnic membership, frequency of meetings, availability of descriptive literature, and
brief description of objectives. Lists over 140 Mexican
American organizations.

325 U.S. Cabinet Committee on Opportunities for the Span-
     ish Speaking. The Spanish Speaking in the United
     States: A Guide to Materials. Washington, D.C.:
     U.S. Gov. Printing Office, 1971. 175p.
   Guide to materials on the Mexican Americans, the
Puerto Ricans, and the Cubans. No division by nationality
but in ten parts including: a listing of books, periodicals
articles, government publications, theses and dissertations,
serials, audiovisual materials, Spanish language radio and
television stations, and subject index. The latter does not
include dissertations or government documents.
   Over 1000 entries and many with approximately ten-
word annotations. Over 256 of these relate to Mexican Americans. These 256 are taken from all disciplines and are iso-
lated in the subject index under Mexican Americans. Like
many other bibliographies, this one has a whimsical selection of works on Mexico that do not relate directly to the
Mexican American. Serials listed refer to Mexican American publications and not indexes or abstracts on this ethnic
group. This bibliography is good for its cross-section of
materials.

326 U.S. Cabinet Committee on Opportunities for the Span-
     ish Speaking. Spanish Surnamed American College
     Graduates. Washington, D.C.: U.S. Gov. Printing
     Office, 1970. 278p.
   Handbook for recruiters of the Spanish surnamed.
Covers 3000 college graduates for 1970. Broad cross-section of training, including candidates for baccalaureate, master's and doctoral degrees from 130 colleges. Individuals
are listed alphabetically by state.

Gives name, address, subject field, degree and date
of graduation.   Also gives breakdown by state of the number
of Spanish surnamed in 15 different disciplines.   (Has a supplement for 1971-1972.)

327 U. S.   Civil Service Commission.   Nosotros hablamos
     español; Federal Employment of Spanish-Speaking Amer-
     icans.   Washington, D. C. :   U. S.   Gov.   Publishing Of-
     fice, 1973.   13p.   C3 1. 48:   Bre-41.
Designed to keep Spanish-surnamed citizens aware of
federal employment opportunities and to help them to compete
for jobs.   Brief introduction on purpose and how Spanish surnamed can take advantage of these services.   Lists 92 job
information centers distributed through the U. S.   Offices are
listed alphabetically by state, then by city.
     This is a directory of federal employment information
put out by the Civil Service Commission.   The purpose is to
encourage the Spanish surnamed to find information by phon-
ing one of the 92 offices and speaking to a representative.
Each entry has complete address and phone number.   Instructions as to purpose and use of this guide are in Spanish and
English.

328 U. S.   Civil Service Commission.   Study of Minority
     Group Employment in the Federal Government, 1965.
     Washington, D. C. :   U. S.   Gov.   Printing Office, 1965.
     193p.
     Presents data on minority employment in the federal
government.   Includes special sections on Negro, Mexican
American, Oriental Americans, American Indians, and Puerto
Ricans, arranged in that order.   Mexican American section
is organized alphabetically by state, i. e. , Arizona, California,
Colorado, New Mexico and Texas.
     Contains approximately 14 pages of statistical tables
on federal employment of Mexican Americans.   Apparently
one of the purposes of this study is to show the increase in
employment over the previous year.   Each of the 13 tables
has: pay category, total employees and Mexican-American
employees for 1965; and change from 1964 of total employees
and Mexican-American employees.   In addition to the Southwestern states, cities of Mexican-American concentration
are also listed.   The study is dated but perhaps now has
value historically for the progress of the Mexican American.

329 U. S. Commission on Civil Rights. Equal Employment
      Opportunity under Federal Law: A Guide to Federal
      Law Prohibiting Discrimination on Account of Race,
      Religion, Sex or National Origin in Private and Public
      Employment. Washington, D. C. , U. S. Gov. Printing
      Office, 1971. 27p.
      Compact information on equal employment and its im-
plications and enforcements--including steps for redress in its
violation. Arranged by general topic--duty of nondiscrimina-
tion, filing a complaint, private employment, public employment, and private or public employment.
      This guide perhaps violates the guidelines established
in the introduction to the present bibliography. However, as
the victims of job discrimination, the Mexican Americans
surely should be made aware of the laws for equal employment and the established machinery for redress. An awareness of their rights as suggested in this guide makes it indispensable in any Chicano collection.

330 U. S. Commission on Civil Rights. Civil Rights Direc-
      tory. Washington, D. C. : U. S. Gov. Printing Office,
      1970. (Clearinghouse Publication No. 15.) 181p.
      Directory to civil rights organizations within the United
States. Includes all racial minority groups. Divided into
five sections, (a) Federal agencies with civil rights responsibilities, (b) Federal agencies with programs of interest to
Spanish-speaking people, (c) National private organizations
with civil rights programs, (d) Official state agencies with
civil rights responsibilities, and (e) Official county and mu-
nicipal agencies with civil rights responsibilities.
      In addition to the section specifically on the Spanish
speaking, Section E lists the names and addresses of 13 organizations interested in civil rights for Mexican Americans
and their contact persons.

331 U. S. Dept. of Agriculture. Economic Research Ser-
      vice. Economic, Social and Demographic Character-
      istics of Spanish-American Wage Workers on U. S.
      Farms. Washington, D. C. : U. S. Gov. Printing Of-
      fice, 1963. (Agriculture Report no. 27.) 21p.
      A survey of Spanish-American wage earners in agri-
cultural employment from 1950 to 1960. This short study is
composed of 18 tables showing education, regional distribution, migratory status, periods of unemployment, etc. Has
content guide showing text and tables.

Perhaps dated now (cut-off, 1960), this study still has value for its succinct coverage of social and demographic characteristics and employment and earnings.

332 U.S. Dept. of Agriculture. Economic Research Service.
     Low-Income Families in the Spanish-Surname Popula-
     tion of the Southwest. Washington, D.C.: U.S. Gov.
     Printing Office, 1967. (Agricultural Economic Report
     no. 112.) 29p.
     Survey of Mexican Americans in the Southwest. Study
includes view of Spanish surname within area compared to the
total population. Number of Mexican born, income, and occupational distribution. Divided into text and charts.
     The 13 tables are the most important part of this
study and include residence, nativity, age, mobility, fertility,
income, labor force, occupation, and education.

333 U.S. Dept. of Agriculture. Economic Research Ser-
     vice. Spanish-Surname Farm Operators in Southern
     Texas. Washington, D.C.: U.S. Gov. Printing Of-
     fice, 1969. (Agriculture Economic Report no. 162.)
     61p.
     A tabular analysis of the farmers in 14 counties of
south Texas, including farms, farm operators and households,
and income from sources other than farms. Has tables of
contents for text and statistics.
     This is a brief survey of the Mexican American farm-
er in one limited area. The text is accompanied by 24
tables and includes such diverse topics as value of livestock
production, level of education, age distribution, etc.

334 U.S. Dept. of Commerce. Bureau of the Census.
     Characteristics of the South and East Los Angeles
     Areas, November, 1965. Washington, D.C.: U.S.
     Gov. Printing Office, 1966. 82p. C3.186:P-23/18.
     Presents a statistical account of the black and Spanish
surnamed population of East Los Angeles. Statistics gathered
in 1965: Race and color, nativity and parentage, household
groups, marital status, education, income, poverty level,
employment status, and housing characteristics. A 12-page
description of survey and its methods and 12 tables compris-
ing the statistical data for the above categories.
     Now dated, this study does give an index to the status
of the Mexican American population of ten years ago in one

of the largest Spanish-speaking cities.   Only the last three
tables focus on the Mexican American.   Except for historical
interest, one should attempt to use the returns for the 1970
census.

335   U. S.   Dept. of Commerce.   Bureau of the Census.
      1970 Census of Population: Persons of Spanish An-
      cestry.   Washington, D. C. :   U. S. Gov. Printing Of-
      fice, 1973.   24p.
      Presents material supplementary to the 1970 census,
i. e. , counts of Spanish ancestry population for the country
as a whole, regions, and states.   In addition, this survey
also includes data on metropolitan areas with more than 5000
persons classified as of Spanish origin.   All material presented in six tables, giving a statistical breakdown of geographical distribution of people of Spanish origin--regions,
states and cities.   Short but useful guide to location of Puerto
Ricans, Mexicans, and Cubans.

336   U. S.   Dept. of Commerce.   Bureau of the Census.
      1970 Census of Population: Persons of Spanish Origin.
      Washington, D. C. :   U. S. Gov. Printing Office, 1974.
      199p.
      Statistics of persons of Spanish origin from the 1970
census.   Tables on origin, rural-urban residence, age, race,
marital status, education, employment status, occupation,
and income.   Also tables are presented on social, economic
and housing characteristics for people of Spanish origin in
cities having between 25, 000 to 50, 000 of this type of population.
      Material abstracted from the 1970 census data on pop-
ulation of Spanish origin.   In addition to the 17 tables, the
study has five appendixes with material on procedures, area
classification, and definition.

337   U. S.   Dept. of Commerce.   Bureau of the Census.
      Persons of Spanish Origin in the United States: No-
      vember 1969.   Washington, D. C. :   U. S. Gov. Print-
      ing Office, 1971.   39p.
      Statistical data on persons of Spanish origin in the
United States.   Includes type of Spanish origin, mother
tongue, language used at home, educational level, literacy,
employment status, occupation group and income.   Divided
into sections that correspond to the above topics.   No index.

Survey based on origin rather than surname. Describes 5 percent of the 200 million people in the United
States, i.e., mainly those of Mexican, Puerto Rican, and
Cuban descent.   Text and 27 tables indicating income, literacy, etc.   Sample for this survey taken from all of the
50 states plus Washington, D.C.   Useful if somewhat dated
guide.

338   U.S.   Dept. of Commerce.   Bureau of the Census.
      Persons of Spanish Origin in the United States.
      March 1972 and 1971.   Washington, D.C.:   U.S. Gov.
      Printing Office, 1973.   34p.
      Current statistics on those of Spanish origin in the
United States: Mexican, Puerto Rican, Cuban, Central or
South American and others of Spanish origin.   Includes demographic, social, economic, and other information on these
groups.   Arranged in text and tables.   Detailed table of contents but no index.
      30 detailed tables on marital status, median income,
years of schooling, age, etc.   Population of Mexican origin
specifically identified in the statistics.

339   U.S.   Dept. of Commerce.   Bureau of the Census.
      Population Characteristics; Selected Characteristics
      of Persons and Families of Mexican, Puerto Rican,
      and Other Spanish Origin.   Washington, D.C.:   U.S.
      Gov. Printing Office, 1971.   19p.
      Presents data on social and economic characteristics
for Mexicans and other Spanish-speaking persons in the
United States.   Includes ethnic origin, age distribution, income, labor force participation, unemployment rates, education, marital status, etc., arranged in that order.   Also contains a guide to tables.
      Basic information on the Mexican American from 1970
census.   This ethnic group specified along with Cuban, Puerto Rican, in tables of statistics with some explanatory text.
Indispensable material.

340   U.S.   Dept. of Commerce.   Office of Minority Business
      Enterprise.   Directory of Minority Media.   Washing-
      ton, D.C.:   U.S. Gov. Printing Office, 1973.   89p.
      C1.2: M66/11
      The purpose of this work is "to avail established and
potential advertisers [of] an additional tool to broaden their

advertising campaigns. " "Media" refers to newspapers, periodicals, radio and television. "Minority" refers to American Indian, Blacks, Oriental Americans, and Spanish-language
Americans. Also has statistical tables of characteristics of
Negro and Spanish heritage population. Arranged by the different media mentioned above and then by minority groups
entered under these separate media.

118 periodicals and newspapers for the Spanish speaking, listed under individual states. Each publication is listed
with address and also 322 radio and tv stations and addresses
for la raza. The final six pages present statistics that would
suggest market potential of Negro and Spanish populations--
age, earnings, rural or urban, etc. Indispensable for the
business man who wants to reach the Spanish heritage market
in the U.S.

341 U.S. Dept. of Commerce. Office of Minority Business
     Enterprise. Higher Education and Aid for Minority
     Business; A Directory of Assistance Available to Min-
     orities by Selected Collegiate Schools of Business.
     Washington, D.C.: U.S. Gov. Printing Office, 1970.
     103p.

Guide to schools of higher education that offer courses
and aid in the field of business for minority groups. Covers
schools offering financial aid to minority students, schools
offering special programs to aid minority business, and
schools offering aid to minorities according to state, arranged in this order. Includes indexes to schools offering
financial aid and those offering special programs.

63 schools offering financial aid: degrees, approxi-
mate costs, financial assistance, special programs, and addresses for admission and financial assistance. Section II
is on schools making steps to aid minority students through
special programs and aids. This guide is presently dated,
but some of its material may still be pertinent to Mexican
Americans interested in business administration.

342 U.S. Dept. of Commerce. Office of Minority Business
     Enterprise. National Directory of Minority Manufac-
     turers, 1974. Washington, D.C.: U.S. Gov. Print-
     ing Office, 1974. 121p.

Designed "to assist procurement personnel in both the
public and private sectors to identify viable minority manufacturing firms that are available for contracting purposes. "
Information probably gathered ca. 1973. "Minority, " in addi-

tion to Mexican American, refers to Indian, Negro, Oriental,
Puerto Rican, etc. Gives companies, products, geographical
area, number of employees, annual sales, type of product,
and ethnic ownership. First 48 pages list 864 minority manufacturers. Last 70 pages comprise five separate indexes for
locating manufacturer by company, by product description,
by geographical location, by standard industrial classification
number, and by federal supply classification number.
     Many Mexican American businesses are listed in this
national directory. To be included, the firm must be 50 per
cent or more owned by minority individuals. Mexican Americans are specifically identified by a code number. The fast-
est way to locate them is by geographical location. This
must be the only guide to Mexican American manufacturers
and its recency, March 1974, makes it useful.

343 U.S. Dept. of Commerce. Office of Minority Business
     Enterprise. National Roster of Minority Consulting
     Professional Firms. Washington, D.C. : U.S. Gov.
     Printing Office, 1973. 121p. C1.57/3:973
          A listing of minority consulting firms to enable them
to receive a fair share of federal contracts. In addition to
Spanish speaking, "minority" also refers to Blacks, Orientals,
American Indians, etc.; all 50 states. Six sections. Alphabetical listing of corporations, company capability statements,
regional index, state index, functional index and general index.
          A consulting firm is one that delivers a report or doc-
ument rather than tangible goods. Minority means that 50
percent or more of the stock is owned by minority group
members. The major section of this work is each firm's
capability statement, which for all 372 firms gives: name,
address, phone, contact, legal structure, date established,
geographic limitation, major areas of expertise and capabil-
ities. Mexican American firms identified only by geographic
location, i.e. , a firm named Valadez in Arizona would be
Mexican American. Useful for locating this type of firm and
probably the only roster in existence on minority consulting
firms.

344 U.S. Dept. of Commerce. Office of Minority Busi-
     ness Enterprise. Special Catalog of Federal Programs
     Assisting Minority Enterprises. Washington, D.C. :
     U.S. Gov. Printing Office, 1971.
          Lists federal programs that provide financial assistance,
business opportunities, management and technical assistance,

sources of trained minority group employees, etc., for minority business enterprise.   Reference chart to type of help offered, descriptions of 85 federal programs, summary of 75
additional federal programs, and regional office location of
agencies who administer these programs.   Covers major federal assistance programs--departments of Agriculture, Commerce, Defense, HEW, Interior, HUD, Justice, Labor,
Treasury, Cabinet Committee on Opportunity for Spanish-
Speaking Peoples, Small Business Administration, TVA, etc.
Appendix and index.
    "Minority" in the title refers also to Spanish speaking.
Each program identified by title, agency, type of help, what
program does, who is eligible, how to apply, helpful reading,
and whom to contact for further information.   A variety of
programs are listed and according to the eligibility requirements, Mexican Americans could apply for many of these.
Excellent indexing.   Main difficulty is that this publication
may now be dated.

345 U.S. Dept. of Health, Education and Welfare.   Bibli-
     ography for Migrant Education Programs.   Washington,
     D.C.:   Educational Systems Corp., 1968.   ERIC ED
     030 052.   108p.
    "This annotated bibliography of curriculum and other
materials is designed primarily to assist consultants and project directors for migrant and seasonal farm worker programs...."   Contains bibliographies on curriculum materials,
testing instruments, cultural materials, education and career
opportunities, social-personal materials, audiovisual materials, bibliographical catalogs, etc., arranged in this order.
Has approximately 600 descriptively annotated entries concerning the phases of migrant education mentioned above.
    Although Mexican Americans are not mentioned, they
are certainly incorporated in the label migrant workers.
This bibliography seems to touch the various skills involved
in migrant education: reading, English as a second language,
social studies, mathematics and vocational.   Has probably
the most variety of any bibliography on migrant education.

346 U.S. Dept. of Health, Education and Welfare.   Cur-
     rent Index to Journals in Education, 1969- .
    This publication relates to Research in Education (see
no. 349), but is devoted entirely to periodical literature in
the field of education.   It is meant to serve the needs of the
educator, reference librarian, and educational researcher.

This monthly publication provides bibliographical control for over 700 publications and other literature related to education. Naturally each issue has references to Mexican Americans and education. As in Research in Education, the user must be aware of the Thesaurus of ERIC Descriptors so that he can find Mexican American under several labels. Each entry has: author, title, journal title and date, descriptors and annotation. Like Research in Education this is valuable for the study of the Mexican American.

347 U. S. Dept. of Health, Education and Welfare. Guide to Audiovisual Aids for Spanish-speaking Americans. Health Related Films, Filmstrips and Slides, Descriptions and Sources. Washington, D. C. : Dept. of HEW, 1973.
     Guide to audiovisual materials in Spanish, mainly films and filmstrips, mid-1950's to early 1970's. Also gives list of distributors. Alphabetized entries under topics. Table of contents but no index.
     Approximately 245 annotated entries on films. Each with title, size, sound, color, length, date of production, purchase and/or rental prices and brief descriptive summary by producers. Material divided under 15 topics, e.g. , accident prevention, aging, diseases and conditions, family planning, etc. Films are in Spanish and for this reason relate to Mexican Americans; however, the health problems presented are universal. One of the best guides to specialized films.

348 U. S. Dept. of Health, Education, and Welfare. Migrant Health Program; Current Operations and Additional Needs. Washington, D. C. : U. S. Gov. Printing Office, 1967. 48p. Y4. L11/2.
     To present an overview of the migrant health problem. Apparently this study assesses what has been done in the five year period, 1962-1967, with the Migrant Health Act. Covers health program goals, areas where migrants are concentrated, homes, health status, health services provided, etc. Arranged similarly to the order suggested above with a few additional topics. Table of contents but no index.
     Highly readable work illustrated with graphs. Usually compares health programs for migrants unfavorably with those for the nation in general. Important capsulated information generally not available in other reference works are mentioned in this bibliography. Mexican Americans are sub-

sumed into the general label "migrant." Yet graphs indicate
that many migrants originate in the Southwest and specifically Texas.

349   U.S.   Dept. of Health, Education and Welfare.   Re-
      search in Education.   1956- .   Monthly.
      This is an abstract journal that announces "completed
research and research-related reports in the field of education." Each monthly issue has subject, author, and institution index. The entries give the following information: title,
descriptors, identifiers, an abstract from 75 to 200 words,
and sources.
      This is an invaluable resource tool for study of the
Mexican American for it contains recent research on the
multiple aspects of education of the Mexican American in
monographs, articles, proceedings and reports. The problem is that the researcher must be thorough in his use of
labels for material on Mexican Americans may be located
under that title or minority group, migrant education, bilingual education, Spanish-speaking, etc. Also has computer
base. See also no. 346.

350   U.S.   Dept. of Health, Education and Welfare.   A
      Study of Selected Socio-Economic Characteristics of
      Ethnic Minorities Based on the 1970 Census.   Volume
      I: Americans of Spanish Origin.   Washington, D.C. :
      HEW, 1970.   118p.
      Presents an analysis of selected data on persons of
Spanish origin from the 1970 census. Covers Mexican Americans, Cuban, and Puerto Rican. Immigration, population
characteristics, family characteristics, education, employment and income, arranged in that order with a table of contents and guide to tables but no index.
      Probably the most recent analysis of the 1970 census
figures. The 13 graphs on Mexican Americans and Puerto
Ricans present statistics on the subjects mentioned above.
Main difference between this and other statistical studies is
the special section in which is abstracted the salient
features of the Mexican American. The 1970 census was
the first one in which citizens of Spanish surname were
further specified as Puerto Rican, Mexican American, etc.
Also according to the introduction, this was an improved
census because emphasis was placed on ethnic/racial minority groups. A pre-census campaign was inaugurated to in-
sure cooperation and Spanish origin rather than Spanish sur-

name was the main designator. In other words, the data
contained in this report should be the most complete and ac-
curate existing.

351   U. S.   Dept. of Health, Education, and Welfare.   Health
      Services and Mental Health Administration.   Spanish-
      Language Health Communication Teaching Aids; A List
      of Printed Materials and Their Sources.   Washington,
      D. C. ?, 1973.   55p.
      A list for individuals and organizations involved in
health activities among Spanish-speaking.   Lists United States
and Puerto Rican organizations and their health oriented publications.   Semi-alphabetized table of contents leads to organizations that distribute materials.   Also subject indexed.
      Guide to 93 organizations that distribute health ori-
ented materials in Spanish.   Organization located by numbered
paragraph and then publications listed.   Includes address of
organization plus short description of publication.   Often titles are bilingual.   Organizations run from the federal government to Alcoholics Anonymous.   Excellent guide that relates
to Mexican Americans because of language.

352   U. S.   Dept. of Health, Education, and Welfare.   Office
      for Civil Rights.   Racial and Ethnic Enrollment Data
      from Institutions of Higher Education, Fall 1970.
      Washington, D. C.   U. S. Gov. Printing Office, 1971?
      205p.   HE 1. 2: R11/970.
      Presents "racial and ethnic enrollment data for insti-
tutions of higher education that responded to HEW's Fall 1970
Civil Rights Survey of Institutions of Higher Education...."
Survey covers the 48 states of the continental United States
and the District of Columbia.   Includes institutions expecting
to receive some form of federal aid.   Minority enrollment
figures for American Indian, Oriental, and Spanish surname.
Arranged alphabetically by state, then by institution.   Medical, dental, and law schools listed separately with state institutions under each.
      Although Mexican Americans are not identified by label,
one can assume that a Spanish surname would indicate this,
at least in Southwest states.   Each institution is presented
with the number of students of each minority group and their
percentage in the total enrollment.   This study, based on students who carry at least three-fourths of a full load, is a
quick indicator as to Mexican American enrollment in the individual institutions.   Useful for potential student who wants

to select an institution where his ethnic group is well repre-
sented.

353   U.S.   Dept. of Health, Education and Welfare.   Office
      of Education.   Office for Spanish-Speaking American
      Affairs.   A Resource List of Spanish Speaking Per-
      sons.   Washington, D.C.:   U.S. Office of Education,
      1973.   48p.
      Alphabetic guide to Spanish surnamed who hold pro-
fessional positions.   Mainly Mexican Americans and Puerto
Ricans who are holders of at least a bachelor's degree.
      No introductory paragraphs as to how selection was
completed for this resource list.   Few non Latin names included, therefore, the title seems misleading.   Approximately
140 entries each with--present title or position, business address and phone, home address and phone, expertise and degree.

354   U.S.   Dept. of Housing and Urban Development.   His-
      panic Americans in the United States: A Selective
      Bibliography, 1963-1974.   Washington, D.C.:   HUD,
      1974.   31p.   ED 096 089
      Cites the most recent print materials on the Mexican
American and the Puerto Ricans.   Includes books, articles,
and bibliographies.   The work is divided into: general background, Mexican Americans, Puerto Ricans and other Caribbean Spanish-speaking peoples, and author index.   Has 328
unannotated entries on materials in English.
      This bibliography is useful because it is recent and it
shows an improvement over earlier government bibliographies
on this topic; e.g., it excludes items on Mexico.   Very good
cross section of Chicano culture.   However, the compilers
do not list any of the Quinto Sol publications nor are they
cognizant of the major works of Chicano poetry.   Surely
imaginative creations would fit within the bibliography's guideline of "insight into their educational, economic, and social
adjustment. "

355   U.S.   Dept. of Housing and Urban Development.   Li-
      brary.   The Mexican Americans: A Bibliography.
      Washington, D.C., 1970.   11p.
      List of books, monographs, and periodicals on Mexi-
can Americans in the library of the Department of Housing
and Urban Development.   Covers all print formats in English

of works published mainly after 1960. Generally in social
science and integrated alphabetically either by author or title.
No index.
   A total of 115 unannotated items. Mainly in social
sciences and education. Naturally lists many Housing and
Urban Development publications on Mexican Americans.

356 U. S. Dept. of Justice. Directory of Organizations
     Serving Minority Communities. Washington, D. C. :
     U. S. Gov. Printing Office, 1971. 88p. J1.2: Or3
   Designed "to provide Department of Justice employers
with names and addresses of some organizations ... that are
involved in serving minority communities. " "Minority" here
refers to women, Negroes, Spanish surname, American Indian, and Oriental. Provides names and addresses of federal
agencies, private organizations, colleges and universities,
newspapers, radio, and tv that serve these minority groups.
Arranges the above minorities separately, first under national
offices, then under local organizations by state. Alphabetized
by state.
   Includes three of the national organizations and 15
state level organizations of Mexican Americans. Only names
and addresses are given and there is no statement of purpose
for each group. Difficult to find in other sources is the listing of the news media in service of the Mexican-American.
An invaluable reference for its unique information.

357 U. S. Dept. of Labor. Directory for Reaching Minority
     Groups. Washington, D. C. : U. S. Gov. Printing Of-
     fice, 1970. 255p.
   Directory of individuals and organizations who are able
to reach minority groups (Blacks, Indians, and Spanish-speaking) to inform them about affirmative action programs. Arranged alphabetically by state, then city.
   Lists approximately 4250 individuals and organizations
in contact with minority groups. Gives name, address,
phone, and position of individuals.

358 U. S. Dept. of Labor. San Juan, Puerto Rico. How
     to Identify Spanish Names. ERIC, 1969. 14p. ED
     031 358
   Discusses the problems involved in identifying Spanish
names. This publication is meant mainly for the government
employee who is unaccustomed to Spanish names. Covers

variations in compound names, suggestions for recording
Spanish names, and forms helpful in determining names.   The
latter also have Spanish translations.
     This work is valuable for any Anglo who is working
with Spanish-speaking people in the United States, for it clari-
fies some of the confusion in Spanish names.   Although most
Mexican Americans have acculturated to Anglo traditions in
names, vestiges of the Spanish system still remain.   Hence
this work is useful to anyone working with the Mexican Americans.   It is also helpful for cultural identity among la raza.

359   U. S.   Dept.   of Labor.   Bureau of Employment Security
      Farm Labor Service.   Information Concerning Entry
      of Mexican Agricultural Workers into the United States.
      Washington, D. C. :   U. S.   Gov.   Printing Office, 1962.
      51p.   L7 35:M57 962
      Guide for potential employers of Mexican nationals in
the United States.   Laws, definitions and multiple aspects of
relationship between employer and Mexican American employees are given.   Has table of contents to the 41 articles of
the migrant Labor Agreement of 1951.
     Brief and perhaps dated, this report does establish
guidelines for the bracero-employer relationship.   All material is highly pertinent--wages, discrimination, strikes, trans-
fer, settlement of claims.   This agreement reads like a list
of goals for an ideal relationship.   Main value is that the
report shows the concern, at least in the abstract, of the
U. S. government for Mexican nationals in the U. S.

360   U. S.   Dept.   of the Navy.   Bureau of Navy Personnel.
      Library Services Branch.   Indian and Mexican Ameri-
      can: A Selective, Annotated Bibliography.   Washing-
      ton, D. C. , 1970.   42p.
      Designed to help navy library personnel develop col-
lections "responsive to the needs of minority and majority
group members. "   Main emphasis is on the American Indian
but seven pages are devoted to the Mexican American.   Divided into short sections of history, labor, sociology, immigration, etc.   Author and title index.
     The 53 annotated entries on Mexican Americans are
a basic list for a core collection on this minority.

361   U. S.   Inter-Agency Committee on Mexican American
      Affairs.   The Mexican American; A New Focus on

Opportunity; A Guide to Materials Relating to Persons
of Mexican Heritage in the United States. Washington,
D. C. : U. S. Gov. Printing Office, 1969. 186p.
A guide mainly to sociological and economic aspects
of la raza. Books, reports, hearings, proceedings, periodical literature, dissertations, bibliographies, audiovisual materials, producers and distributors, and Spanish-language
radio t. v. Arranged in that order, with surname entered
alphabetically under each category. No index.
One of the most complete bibliographies for its period
for the subject areas suggested. Has categories of materials
often excluded from other bibliographies--e. g. , reports,
hearings, proceedings that rarely appear in most Chicano
bibliographies. Yet here are listed almost 325 such ephem-
eral items. Also are included 30 pages of unpublished materials and 40 pages of radio and t. v. stations. The periodical literature and books could be found in most standard
bibliographies.

362 University of California, Davis. University Library.
     Collection Development Section. Ethnic Studies Unit.
     Chicano Bibliography by Davis Chapter of this Movi-
     miento Estudiantil Chicano de Aztlán. Davis: Uni-
     versity of California Library, 1965. 51p.
     Guide to Chicano materials in the library of the uni-
versity. Monographs and articles on Mexican Americans and
Mexico. Alphabetized by main entry under 21 separate categories. No index, but table of contents.
     Over 1000 unannotated entries. Although some of the
subject categories are extremely useful, e. g. , bracero scene,
health of Mexican Americans and el movimiento Chicano, too
many categories are purely Mexican, e. g. , Aztec, Zapoteca,
Conquest, etc. No guidelines are given as to inclusion criteria. A new edition of this came out in 1969 but has no
major changes from the original.

363 University of California, Los Angeles. Chicano Studies
     Center. Early Childhood Education: A Selected Bib-
     liography. Los Angeles: Chicano Research Library
     of the Chicano Studies Center, 1972. 30p.
     Collects articles and books on childhood education.
Includes more than Mexican Americans and relates to early
development and ethnic groups in general. Arranged by format. No annotations and no index.
     Approximately 300 unannotated entries that cover child-

hood education with a focus on Mexican Americans. Includes
writers on bilingualism, the culturally different, and a discussion of headstart program.

364 University of California, Los Angeles. Chicano Studies
     Center and Instructional Media Library. Film Collec-
     tion of the Chicano Research Library and Instructional
     Media Library. Los Angeles: University of California,
     1973. 10p.
     Guide to Chicano and related films at UCLA. Films
only, arranged alphabetically. Probably all were produced in
the last ten years.
     Lists 23 film titles, each with a descriptive annota-
tion. Only four of these are Mexican American; the remaining 19 are generally of a social protest type. Since these
are for rent, the price is given. Unfortunately the date of
the film is not included. Since the purpose is to rent films,
the evaluations are not always objective. This film list could
be used in conjunction with the two works of Cynthia Baird
(both q.v.).

365 University of California, Los Angeles. Institute of In-
     dustrial Relations. Directory of Organizations in
     Greater Los Angeles. Los Angeles: UCLA, 1973.
     186p.
     A guide to organizations for "persons concerned about
social and economic problems in this area" (i.e., south
central and east Los Angeles). Apparently covers all of Los
Angeles up to April 1973 but with an emphasis on the areas
stated above. Includes organizations and associations related
to civil and legal rights, religion, community and neighbor-
hood, business assistance, research and referral, government
agencies, politics, services and fraternity, labor, communication and legal services, arranged in this order. Under
each type of association, entries are arranged according to
the area in Los Angeles in which organization is located.
Table of contents and index to organization.
     Invaluable guide for Mexican Americans needing speci-
fied services. Under each type of association are usually
listed several groups whose main concern is the Mexican
American. Entries include area locations, address, director,
phone number and a paragraph describing function and purposes. Other minority groups mentioned besides Mexican
and Americans.

366 University of California, Los Angeles. Mexican-American Study Project. Revised Bibliography. Los Angeles: UCLA Graduate School of Business Administration, Division of Research, 1967. (Advance Report
3.) 99p.
Intended to simplify and update the 1966 bibliography
by ignoring chronological categories and by reducing the categories from 12 to five. Covers Mexican Americans in books,
journal articles, unpublished master's and doctoral dissertations, and other unpublished materials. All aspects of Mexican American culture. Arranged by the above mentioned
formats. No index.
One of the better Mexican American bibliographies because of its scope; it lists approximately 390 books and 578
unannotated journal articles. Besides the traditional material, this bibliography includes more on government publications and missionary efforts among Mexican Americans. Also has one of the more complete listings of theses and dissertations. The lack of an index makes use somewhat cum-
bersome.

367 University of California, Santa Barbara. Chicanos: A
Selective Guide to Materials in the University of California at Santa Barbara. Santa Barbara, n. p. , 1972.
78p.
Guide to Mexican American holdings in UCSB--books,
curriculum development guides, and government publications.
No periodical articles. Entries are alphabetized under subject categories. Has a personal name index and a subject
index.
772 unannotated entries are easy to find with the two
indexes. Certainly one of the better bibliographies of a single library's holdings. One of its main assets is the section
on curriculum in which 44 studies related to this are listed.
Main problem is lack of statement of limits as to what should
be incorporated under chicanismos. For example, many
works from Mexico are listed and some well known works by
Anglos are excluded.

368 University of Houston. Libraries. Mexican Ameri-
cans: A Selected Bibliography Revised and Enlarged,
Fall 1974. Houston, Texas: University of Houston
Libraries, 1974. 151p.
A guide to the library holdings for Mexican American
studies. Includes books, journals and newspapers, audio-

visual materials and bibliographies. Cross-section of all aspects of Chicano life: history, sociology, labor, politics, education, literature, fine arts, and biography. Arranged by these subdivisions; has author/main entry index, but no subject index.

This is one of the better examples of a catalog of one library's holdings on Mexican Americans. It is current because (apparently) this is the second edition. Has approximately 1450 unannotated entries of material on Mexican Americans, Spain and Mexico, and general items such as Oscar Handlin's The Uprooted. Excellent cross-section on Mexican Americans even though some of the items on Mexico seem extremely peripheral. The section on literature is one of the best developed in any bibliography of this nature for it includes Mexican works, Chicano self portrayal and Anglo interpretation of Chicanos.

369 University of New Mexico. Zimmerman Library. New Titles and Additions, vol. 4, no. 10. Albuquerque, N.M.: Zimmerman Library, Ethnic Studies Dept., October, 1974. 8p.

An attempt to keep bibliographies current on ethnic studies at the University of New Mexico. African, Black, Chicano, and Native American Studies. Mainly monographs but also some articles--from 1955 to 1974. Entries alphabetized under group.

There are 19 entries occasionally annotated on Mexican Americans. To be completely useful, the entire series would have to be studied. However, this is an excellent method for maintaining currency in a bibliography from the largest library in New Mexico.

370 University of Texas at Austin. Mexico American Student Directory, 1974-1975. Austin: Ethnic Student Services, 1975? 64p.

Directory of Mexican American students, staff, faculty, and organizations at the University of Texas. In addition to names, also has pertinent information on student services and Chicano related programs. Arranged in the sections suggested above. Table of contents.

Probably the most complete guide to chicanismo at the University of Texas. Apparently the compilers were careful to incorporate only those Spanish surnamed who could be identified as Mexican American, and the Spanish surname itself was not a limiting factor as some Anglo names are included. Has pictures and some poetry.

371   University of Texas at Austin.   Center for Mexican-
      American Studies.   Mexican-Americanists of Texas:
      A Chicano Studies Directory.   Austin, 1971.   17p.
      A guide to Mexican-Americanists to aid communica-
tion among all Texas Chicanos.   Apparently this directory includes only the participants at the Institute on Mexican-American Studies held at the University of Texas in 1970.   Lists
alphabetically approximately 170 Mexican-Americanists.   Includes profession and place of employment, address, and
brief description of Mexican American activities.

372   University of Texas at Austin.   Institute of Latin Ameri-
      can Studies.   Seventy-Five Years of Latin American
      Research at the University of Texas.   Austin, 1959?
      Lists all master's theses and doctoral dissertations,
1893-1958, and publications of Latin American interest, 1941-
1958, in the University library.   Arranged chronologically,
then alphabetically by author.   Index of authors and topics.
      Lists 670 theses and dissertations with minimal bib-
liographical information.   Many, mainly in education, relate
to Mexican Americans.

373   University of Utah.   Marriott Library.   Chicano Bibli-
      ography.   Salt Lake: University of Utah, 1973.   (Bib-
      liographic Series, vol. I.)   295p.
      Enables researchers to have access to Mexican Amer-
ican materials in the University of Utah libraries.   Includes
monographs, government documents, curriculum collection of
Marriott Library, selections from Educational Resource Information Center, periodicals and films, arranged in that
order.   No index.
      Approximately 2950 unannotated entries.   No guide-
lines are presented as to limits to definition of Chicano materials, except the (earliest) date 1846.   Perhaps most unique
aspect is section on children's literature.   Lack of index less-
ens utility of this bibliography.

374   University of Utah.   Marriott Library.   Behavioral Sci-
      ences Library.   A Selective Chicano Bibliography of
      Materials at the University of Utah.   Salt Lake City:
      University of Utah Libraries, 1971.   93p.
      Guide to Chicano materials in the Marriott Library
at the University of Utah.   Books, periodicals, pamphlets,
microforms and films.   "Chicano" in the title refers to Span-

ish Americans, American Indians, Cubans, Puerto Ricans,
and Eskimos living within the United States. No government
documents. Arranged alphabetically by format. Books are
subdivided by topic.
   The scope of this bibliography is too encompassing.
Therefore, very few of the entries pertain to the Mexican
Americans. Annotations appear only for articles listed in
Education Index, a cumulative topical index to certain periodicals in education, and to proceedings and yearbooks.

375 University of Washington. Library School Association.
     Chicano Related Materials in the University of Wash-
     ington Library: A Selected Bibliography. Seattle:
     Library School Assoc., 1970. 74p.
   A guide to some of the Chicano materials in this li-
brary--all print materials in all formats. Social sciences,
history, and literature mainly in government documents,
theses, monographs, and periodicals, dealing with Mexican
Americans and also Mexicans. Arranged alphabetically by
author. No table of contents or index.
   This is one of the larger bibliographies of Chicano-
related materials in one library. It has over 800 entries,
unannotated, with basic bibliographic information plus the
call number. The work is inter-disciplinary but reflects the
usual confusion on incorporation of items on Mexico. It has
no introductory essay that would establish guidelines. The
lack of an index frustrates the user and necessitates scanning
the entire bibliography to find pertinent items. This bibliography is seriously in need of updating and reorganization.
The copy evaluated was obtained from the University of Washington Library.

376 Vasquez, Librado Keno, and Maria Enriqueta Vasquez.
     Regional Dictionary of Chicano Slang. Austin, Texas:
     Jenkins Pub. Co., 1975. 111p.
   According to the authors, the purpose of this dictionary is to provide "an easy tool of Oral communication in Bar-
riology Terminology." The vocabulary is taken from various
Chicano dialects: Tex-Mex, Caló, Pachuquismo, and Cali-
Mex. Divided into several sections: author's explanation,
introduction, pronunciation guide, abbreviations, vocabulary,
Chicano-Hispano-Americano phrases, bibliography, proverbs
and sayings, riddles, Chicano folk medicine, Chicano folk-
songs, and an English-Chicano-Hispano index. Compilers list
approximately 1500 words of regional derivation. Each entry

has correct spelling, definition in English, and then coding
to indicate region where used.
    This is an attractive work that contains much of the
Mexican American as expressed in his own vocabulary. However, it would have been more useful with pronunciation, part
of speech, use in context, and, when possible, etymology.
The compilers mention nothing on methodology for gathering
these words. What classifies a word as standard Spanish and
what criteria relegate it to the deprecatory category of slang?
No mention is made in either the introduction or the bibliography of an awareness of similar studies, e.g., Blanco S.,
Cerda, Coltharp (all q.v.). In spite of defects this work is
one of the first commercial Chicano dictionaries that will
hopefully lead to more expanded ones. This copy obtained
at Trinity University.

377 Vassberg, David E. Bibliography of Materials Relating
     to the Use of Mexican and Mexican-American Agricul-
     tural Labor in the Lower Rio Grande Valley of Texas
     [mimeographed]. Austin, Texas, 196? 21ℓ.
    An attempt to list all publications for the topic men-
tioned in the title. Has primary sources--memoirs, autobi-
ographies, etc.; secondary sources--monographs, theses, and
dissertations; sources published by state and federal govern-
ments; fiction, miscellaneous sources and published bibliographies. Excludes periodicals. Arranged in above order. No
table of contents or index.
    Lists approximately 150 entries, mainly unannotated.
No introduction to guide reader or to outline the scope of the
work. Makes no mention of archives and gives no reason
for excluding periodicals. An index would have made the
work more useful. Some basic works, like Browning, Elac,
and Schmidt (all q.v.) not mentioned. However, this is one
of the few bibliographies on a social science topic that includes works of fiction.

378 Villarreal, Roberto M. Farm Workers and the Mini-
     mum Wage. Austin, Texas: National Migrant Informa-
     tion Clearing House, 1974. 16p.
    "Present[s] the reader with the facts with regard to
the extension of the Federal Minimum Wage to all farmworkers." Covers the legislative background, the minimum wage
today, issues of minimum wages, and extension of minimum
wage coverage to farmworkers. Arranged in this order.
    Highly condensed discussion of the minimum wage for

farmworkers.   Most valuable is the section of the minimum
wage laws by state.   Relates to the Mexican American who
is part of the migrant labor stream.

379   Villarreal, Roberto M.   Workmen's Compensation; Guide
      for Farmworkers.   Austin, Texas: National Migrant
      Information Clearing House, 1974.   21p.
      Guide for farm and agricultural workers and for groups
or individuals who want to assist them in understanding workmen's compensation.   Provides definition of workmen's compensation, coverage by state, reasons for this type of compensation, deficiencies of workmen's compensation and some
alternatives, and workmen's compensation requirements ap-
plicable to injured workers.
      A brief study on workmen's compensation, the pro-
gram that provides cash benefits and medical aid to victims
of work injuries.   Main reference value is the chart on coverage by state.   Each of 50 states outlined as to status of
compensation--compulsory, voluntary, prohibited--and comments as to peculiarities of the various state laws.   This is
relevant to Mexican American migrant farm workers as this
occupational group has largely been excluded from compulsory
state compensation laws.   Also valuable is the chart with
data presented state by state as to the formalities involved
in making a claim.

380   Wagner, Henry R.   Bibliography of Works Bearing on
      the History of Those Portions of the United States
      which Formerly Belonged to Mexico.   Santiago, Chile:
      La Imprenta Diener, 1917.   43p.
      Presents works on the Southwestern U.S.A. abstracted
from compilations of the famous Chilean bibliographer, José
Toribio Medina.   Covers books and pamphlets in Spanish only
published from 1553 to 1821.   Entries are chronological.
      137 works from the bibliographies of one of the world's
most famous bibliographers.   Each entry has collation, publication date, and citation of sources.   The works are not annotated but the lengthy titles are a primitive form of annotation.   Includes books on establishment of missions, travel,
history, etc.   Must be one of the few bibliographies of books
in Spanish on the Southwestern United States and therefore indispensable for serious study of Mexican American roots in
the colonial period.

381   Wagner, Henry R.   The Spanish Southwest, 1542-1794;
      An Annotated Bibliography.   Albuquerque, N. M. :
      Quivira Society, 1937.   2 vols.
      Guide to works published 1542-1794 referring to those
parts of the United States that formerly belonged to Mexico.
Entries mainly in Spanish and English.   In addition to Southwestern United States, there are references to Coahuila and
Sonora.   Arranged chronologically except in the case of later
editions so they could be grouped.   Mainly author index but
some subject.
      The author has availed himself of the most fruitful
sources in order to compile this bibliography, e. g. , José
Toribio Medina, the British Museum, the Bibliothèque Na-
tionale in Paris, the Biblioteca Nacional in Madrid, the
Archivo General de las Indias in Seville, etc.   Of the 177
annotated entries, many refer to California, New Mexico and
Texas.   Each entry has collation, discrepancies of various
editions, sources regarding printings and translations, and
some biographical data.   Important for the Spanish heritage
of Mexican Americans.

382   Wallace, Ernest, and David M. Vigness.   Documents of
      Texas History.   Austin, Texas: Steck Co. , 1963.
      293p.
      Source book of materials "worthy of preservation" on
Texas history.   Documents taken from all of Texas history,
1528 to 1961, often inaccessible to students.   Table of contents and topical index.
      Gives the essence of 126 documents, chronologically
arranged.   Each is preceded by a short introduction that provides the context of the document and its source.   Relates
to Mexican American for its inclusion of their roots in Texas
--i. e. , the Spanish settlement, the War with Mexico and others perhaps more peripheral.

383   Whitney, Philip.   America's Third World: A Guide to
      Bibliographic Resources in the Library of the Univer-
      sity of California, Berkeley.   Berkeley: University
      of California General Library, 1970.   89ℓ.
      Guide to United States ethnic minorities at Berkeley.
"Third World" means Africans, Asians, Latin Americans and
Native Americans within the United States.   Both separates
and analytics.   Arranged alphabetically by subject headings
according to those prescribed by the Library of Congress.
No index.

Mainly on Negroes.   Very difficult to use because
Mexican Americans may be found under several subject headings, which necessitates perusing the entire work to find
pertinent entries.   No annotations.

384   Winnie, William W. Jr., John F. Stegner, and Joseph
      P. Kopachevsky. Persons of Mexican Descent in the
      United States: A Selected Bibliography. Fort Collins:
      Colorado State University, Center for Latin American
      Studies, 1970.   78p.
         Designed to assist the scholar interested in social sci-
ence research on Mexicans in the United States from 1891 to
1970.   Anthropology, economics, psychology, political science
and sociology in monographs and periodical articles.   Theses
and dissertations included are from the state of Colorado
only.   Inaccessible items excluded.   Arranged alphabetically
by author.   No indexing.   Bibliographies listed separately.
         Approximately 1000 unannotated entries.   Criterion
for incorporation was "only items which supply content of
importance...."   All unpublished manuscripts were eliminated.
The lack of an index makes this work difficult to use.

385   Wright, Doris Marion.   A Guide to the Mariano Guada-
      lupe Vallejo Documentos para la Historia de California,
      1780-1875.   Berkeley: University of California Press,
      1955.   264p.
         A guide to "one of the most important collections of
primary source materials for the Mexican period of California
history."   10,000 manuscripts in 36 volumes.   Letters and
other documents of many men prominent in California during the early to mid-19th century.   Documents entered
chronologically under author surname.   No index.
         This collection belonged originally to Mariano Guada-
lupe Vallejo, Comandante General of California.   Contains
information on government and politics, military history,
missions, economic history, immigration, colonization, and
social history.   In other words, this is a guide to a unique
source for California history--the Mexican period.   Scholars
interested in Mexican American history and genealogy would
find it valuable.   Each manuscript is listed under name of
author; also has the name of the person addressed, the date
and place of writing, and a descriptive word to define the
document.

386   Zelayeta, Elena Emilia.   Elena's Fiesta Recipes.   Los
      Angeles: Ward Ritchie Press, 1961. 126p.
      Collection of party recipes of Mexican, American and
European origin.   Not basic foods but mainly fiesta dishes.
Has table of contents and index.
      Approximately 240 recipes.   Some Mexican but more
international in scope than Elena's Mexican and Spanish Recipes (see following entry).   Very careful instructions for
preparing Mexican dishes in the U.S.   Not a first choice and
definitely inferior to her other mentioned above.

387   Zelayeta, Elena Emilia.   Elena's Mexican and Spanish
      Recipes.   Englewood Cliffs, N.J.:   Prentice Hall,
      1961.   127p.
      Presents the author's conception of Mexican food as it
is enjoyed in the United States.   Basic Mexican recipes and
menus for typical Mexican meals.   Book divided into 14 sections, e.g., soups, eggs, meats, etc.   Table of contents but
no index.
      The author of this book, a Mexican living in California,
has adapted the recipes to the availability of ingredients in
the U.S.   Because of her residence in California, Zelayeta's
book may be classified as a California-Mexican cookbook.
Approximately 375 recipes that regionally relate to California.
1961 was the 58th printing of this work.

AUTHOR INDEX

TITLE INDEX
(includes titles cited in annotations)

The Romance of Spanish Surnames 188

SUBJECT INDEX

abstracts 22, 40, 93, 136, 151,
171, 173, 208, 235, 245,
249, 294, 349
academic achievement 151
Academy of American Francis-
can History 58
Academy of California Church
History 266
accounts 58
acculturation 219, 267
adult education 57, 114; see
also adults
adult literature 84, 124, 250
adults 66, 70, 132, 250, 291
advertisers 340
Affirmative Action Programs
199, 241, 357
age 333, 336, 339
aged 148, 189, 338, 339
agriculture 95, 103, 144, 154,
155, 162, 198, 203, 216,
231, 239, 282, 286, 288,
299, 303, 331, 333, 345,
359, 378, 379
agriculture--bibliography 107,
144
agriculture--statistics 103, 333
alabado 46
Alameda County, Calif. 134
Alavez, Francita "Panchita" 202
alien commuters 154
almanacs 308
American Baptist Church 87
Anglos 38, 54, 63, 83, 89,
102, 113, 120, 121, 126,
163, 176, 236, 243, 244,
246, 276, 278, 280, 313,
314, 368, 370
anthologies 70, 230
anthropology 65, 118, 189, 207,
235, 244, 384; see also social
science

archaisms 165, 186
Archdiocese of Santa Fe 58
architecture 277, 288
archives 26, 38, 51, 52, 56,
58, 62, 78, 96, 127, 140,
141, 142, 143, 166, 217,
234, 261, 274, 285, 304,
309, 321; see also depositories; documents; manuscripts
Archivo General de las Indias
381
Archivo Historical Nacional 285
Argentina 7
Arizona 16, 18, 29, 56, 61,
63, 87, 101, 139, 143, 174,
180, 191, 216, 222, 224,
243, 290, 300, 313, 318,
328
Arizona--archive 143
Arizona--history 139, 174,
318
Arizona Historical Society 63
Armacost Library, Univ. of
Redlands 260
arts 119, 150, 157, 251, 255,
269, 281, 284, 298, 368;
see also individual art forms
arts--bibliography 145
assimilation see acculturation
attorneys see lawyers
audiotapes 237; see also audiovisual materials
audiovisual materials 29, 33,
39, 77, 84, 85, 98, 144,
150, 157, 167, 170, 196,
202, 228, 231, 237, 244,
248, 251, 301, 303, 307,
323, 325, 345, 347, 364
audiovisual materials--bibliogra-
phy 170, 347, 361
Austin, Texas 9, 159, 210,
309, 378, 379

176